Fundamentals of Genealogy®: Basics f ⌐ne

Second edition, part of the *Fundamentals of Genealogy*® te

A quick reference guide to accreditea .. research strategies, U.S. record groups and more.

Basic Genealogical Concepts, Kinship Calculator, Charts, DNA Testing & More

Important U.S. Public & Private Sources . . . *and how to find more sources*

Basic U.S. Genealogical Record Groups

- ❧ **"Beginning Genealogy** - How Do I Get Started?"
- ❧ **"Brick Walls** – Strategies For Breaking Thru"
- ❧ **"Conflicting Information** - How Do I Resolve It?"
- ❧ **"Female Ancestors** – Researching For Maiden Names"
- ❧ **"First Finding Sources"**
- ❧ **"Immigrant Ancestor's Birthplace** - How Do I Begin Research To Find It?"
- ❧ **"New Year's Resolution Suggestions"**
- ❧ **"Newly Found Ancestor** - How Do I Begin Research On A Newly Found Ancestor?"
- ❧ **"No Initial Information** – How Do I Begin Researching If I Have Virtually No Initial Info?"
- ❧ **"Notetaking Software** – A Format To Quicken, Organize And Record Your Research"
- ❧ **"Notetaking Software** - Using A Research Template"
- ❧ **"Rounding Up The Usual Suspects"**
- ❧ **"Rounding Up BEYOND The Usual Suspects"**

- ❧ Suggestions for dealing with a common question, **"What do I do next?"**
- ❧ Suggestions for dealing with another common question, **"Where do I go next?"**

Second Edition, ISBN 978-0-578-18416-6

Fundamentals of Genealogy® textbook series, Post Office Box 832, Wilmette, Illinois 60091-0832 USA

Publisher: Marsha Peterson-Maass || **Illustrator:** Bill Maass

BASIC GENEALOGICAL CONCEPTS, KINSHIP CALCULATOR, CHARTS, DNA TESTING & MORE

Checklist
***Fundamentals of Genealogy*® Start With Accredited Methods**
#1–Understand accredited research methodology *Genealogy, the pursuit of finding one's ancestry, is more than just writing names on a family tree – it's finding the documented pieces of your ancestors' lives that they left behind. We use an accredited methodology because there's a science behind the process. We rely on credible sources plus clear & convincing evidence to substantiate proof that ultimately gives us reliable conclusions. Why? Because we're in the pursuit of truth.***1**
The National Genealogical Society's "**Guidelines for Sound Genealogical Research**" www.ngsgenealogy.org/cs/ngs_guidelines
The Accredited Method dictates that we properly identify each individual, then move back one generation at a time to prove the identities of each pair of parents, building the proven lineage backward one generation at a time.
Familiarize yourself with the following accredited methodology (pages 3-22): • *Chapter 1, "**Basic Genealogical Concepts, Kinship Calculator, Charts, DNA Testing & More**" including, "**Basic Accredited Genealogical Standards and Methods for Research & Planning**" (page 6).*
#2–Places for recording and storing your records
National Genealogical Society's "**Guidelines for Use of Computer Technology in Gen. Research**" www.ngsgenealogy.org/cs/ngs_guidelines
Set up the following three recording and organizing solutions: • "**Summary of Genealogical Software**" (page 81) • *Fundamentals of Genealogy*® **Research Strategy, "Notetaking Software**" (page 105) • "*Fundamentals of Genealogy*® **Organizational Challenge**" (pages 82-87)
#3–Gather your family information
Gather the family information you already have, contact relatives to collect their information, list their family heirlooms and schedule interviews . . . *see* "**Family Sources (including How To Interview Family)**" (page 23). • Make an inventory of your family's precious heirlooms.
Begin recording information you already have and **begin citing** your sources in the accredited methodology (pages 79-81). Record it on paper or a notetaking software program and begin adding it to your family tree . . . see "**Fundamentals of Genealogy®: Recording Style Sheet**" (page 80).

---

1 Board for Certification of Genealogists, ***The BCG Genealogical Standards Manual***, (Washington, D.C., U.S.A.: Ancestry Publishing, 2014), 1-19.

	• Especially as a beginner, remember when you collect info from any source you need to get as much location information as possible, including place names for when your ancestor lived there and what it's called today.
#4–Research, Analyze, Record & Organize using accredited methods	

	Focus on researching one ancestor to **prove their Identity** (page 6). To then build a biographical portrait of their life, use the **Ancestral Profile** (pages 7-8). And follow this **<u>Accredited Research and Planning Process</u>**:
	• **"Identify Each Ancestor To Individualize Them"** (page 6)
	• **"Think Like a Genealogist"** (page 6)
	• **"Methodology-Strategy-Locating Cycle"** (page 6)
	• **"Important U.S. Public & Private Sources"** (pages 24-31)
	• **"Basic U.S. Genealogical Record Groups"** (pages 32-68)
	• **"Some Basic Genealogical Tools"** (page 69-75)
	• **"Checklist For The Genealogical Analysis Process"** (page 76) and *"Fundamentals of Genealogy®: Analysis Style Sheet"* (pages 77-78)
	• *"Fundamentals of Genealogy®: Recording Style Sheet"* (page 80)
	  • **"Checklist For Recording Process"** Citation of Sources (page 79)
	• *"Fundamentals of Genealogy®: Organizational Challenge"* (pp 82-87)
	• **Planning including Research Strategies** (pages 100-106)
	  • "Beginning Genealogy - How Do I Get Started?" (pages 100-101)
	  • "Newly Found Ancestor - How Do I Begin Research On A Newly Found Ancestor?" (page 104)
	  • "Rounding Up the Usual Suspects" (page 106)

	Follow up your initial research with: • **"Networking"** (pages 88-92) • **"Preservation"** (pages 92-95) • **"Presentations"** (pages 95-98)
#5–Educate yourself further	
	National Genealogical Society's **"Guidelines for Genealogical Self-Improvement & Growth"** <u>www.ngsgenealogy.org/cs/ngs_guidelines</u>
	See **"Recommended Educational Resources"** (page 29-31)
	See **"Important U.S. Genealogical & Historical Societies"** (page 29)
	See **Appendix A: Your Own Genealogical Library** (page 100)
#6–Share your research results	
	The National Genealogical Society's **"Guidelines for Sharing Information with Others"** <u>www.ngsgenealogy.org/cs/ngs_guidelines</u>
	Share research + heirlooms with relatives in at least digital form (pp 95-98)
	See **"Networking"** (pages 88-92)
	See **"Presentations"** (page 95-98)
	See *"Fundamentals of Genealogy®: The Most Helpful Tools You've Never Used.*

<u>*Fundamentals of Genealogy*® 9-Essential Elements Of The Genealogical Process</u> . . . *Every genealogist's ultimate goal should be to achieve the Board for Certification of Genealogists'* **"Genealogical Proof Standard[1]**,*" which simply put means, ". . . to assemble (and perhaps share with others) a reconstructed family history that is as close to the truth as possible." To achieve this goal, we practice the 9-Essential Elements of the Genealogy Process (along with the "NGS Guidelines"[2]) to measure the credibility of our statements in our pursuit of the truth.*

<u>Element #1—Education:</u> We gain as thorough and scholarly an understanding of the genealogy process elements as possible thru education, networking, etc.

<u>Element #2—Research Cycle:</u> "We conduct a reasonably exhaustive search in reliable sources for all information that is or may be pertinent to the identity, relationship, event, or situation in question." The research cycle includes:
Prep Work ~ Research Plan ~ Research Activity~ Research Activity Log**.**

<u>Element #3—Collection:</u> "We collect and include in our compilation a complete, accurate citation to the source or sources of each item of information we use."

<u>Element #4—Analysis:</u> "We analyze and correlate the collected information to assess its quality as evidence."

<u>Element #5—Resolution:</u> "We resolve any conflicts caused by items of evidence that contradict each other or are contrary to a proposed (hypothetical) solution."

<u>Element #6—Proving:</u> We are not required to produce "proof beyond the shadow of a doubt," but instead by "clear and convincing evidence." When new evidence surfaces or flaws in the conclusion are found, we re-examine the statement to determine if it remains valid."

<u>Element #7—Recording:</u> We practice timely, accurate recording of all analyzed evidence along with source citations, in all necessary recording media, like research logs, ancestral database software programs, forms and charts, etc.

<u>Element #8—Organization:</u> We responsibly file, store and restore all ancestral documentation and heirlooms in an organized fashion as to preserve them far into the future, and to locate them for any future genealogical use.

<u>Element #9—Presentation:</u> "We arrive at a soundly reasoned, coherently written conclusion." We present only that evidence which meets the Genealogical Proof Standard in a clear and accurate way. We use fully source-cited genealogical compilations, like research reports, proof summaries, lineages, pedigrees, etc.

---

1 Board for Certification of Genealogists' **The BCG Genealogical Standards Manual**, (Washington, District of Columbia, U.S.A.: Ancestry Publishing, 2014), 1-19.

2 (U.S.) National Genealogical Society's **"NGS Guidelines,"** second edition (Arlington, Virginia, U.S.A.: National Genealogical Society, 2016). https://www.ngsgenealogy.org/cs/ngs_guidelines

Fundamentals of Genealogy® Research & Planning Methodology . . .
Use these three accredited methods as part of the "#4–Research, Analyze, Record & Organize using accredited methods" on page 4.

🌿 **"Identify Each Ancestor To Individualize Them"**
To "identify" your ancestor, collect evidence that distinguishes them from every other person who ever lived ("individualization"). At a minimum:
- **Full name** *(including nicknames, maiden name, spellings, etc.)*
- **Dates and locations of vital events** *(birth, marriage, divorce, death)*
- **Proof of parentage** *(at least 2 sources stating a parental relationship)*
  - Record types that often state a parental relationship --- Biography, Home sources, Land, Lineage, Military, Obituary, U.S. Social Security, Vital records, Wills/Probate, etc.

🌿 **"Think Like a Genealogist"** . . . the 3 Contextual Frames
Place your ancestor in the 3 Contextual Frames each time you research.
- **Frame #1** – Identify the **PERSON** (see "Identify" above).
- **Frame #2** – Put the correct person in the correct **LOCATION**.
- **Frame #3** – Put the correct person in the correct location during the correct **TIME PERIOD**.

🌿 **Methodology-Strategy-Locating Cycle** . . . overcoming the 3 Q's
This is how you formulate your Research Plan!
- **Methodology** - "How do I know that I need a record?"
  → → → Use the **Ancestral Profile** (pages 7-8).
- **Strategy** - "How do I know whether a record exists?
  → → → Use the **Research Strategies** (Appendix B).
  - 🌿 **"Beginning Genealogy** - How Do I Get Started?"
  - 🌿 **"Female Ancestors** – Researching For Maiden Names"
  - 🌿 **"First Finding Sources"**
  - 🌿 **"Immigrant Ancestor's Birthplace** - How Do I Begin Research To Find It?"
  - 🌿 **"Newly Found Ancestor** - How Do I Begin Research On A Newly Found Ancestor?"
  - 🌿 **"No Initial Information** – How Do I Begin Researching If I Have Virtually No Info?
  - 🌿 **"Notetaking Software** – A Format To Quicken, Organize And Record Your Research"
  - 🌿 **"Notetaking Software** - Using A Research Template"
  - 🌿 **"Rounding Up the Usual Suspects"**
  - 🌿 **"Rounding Up BEYOND the Usual Suspects"**
- **Locating** - "How do I know where to find a record?"
  → → → Use "**Basic U.S. Genealogical Record Groups**" (pages 32-68) and "**Important U.S. Public & Private Sources**" (pages 23-31).

Fundamentals of Genealogy®: Basics for Everyone

Second edition, part of the *Fundamentals of Genealogy*® textbook series

---

Ancestral Profile for (Name) _____ **Fan Chart #** _____

Vital Records (Birth, Marriage, Divorce & Death)
Birth Date, Location & Source _____

_____

Baptism Date, Location & Source _____
☐ *Baptismal Record* ☐ *Biographical Sources* ☐ *Birth Certificate* ☐ *Census Records* ☐ *Death Certificate*
☐ *Military Files* ☐ *Naturalization Application* ☐ *Obituary* ☐ *Passport Application* ☐ *Social Security Records*

Marriage Date, Location & Source _____
Name of Spouse(s) _____
Name of Institution _____
☐ *Biographical Sources* ☐ *Cemetery Info* ☐ *Census Records* ☐ *Death Certificate* ☐ *Family Records*
☐ *Marriage Certificate* ☐ *Military Files* ☐ *Obituary* ☐ *Religious Marriage Records* ☐ *Will & Probate*

Date of Divorce_____ **Court Location & Source**_____
☐ *Biographical Sources* ☐ *Census Records* ☐ *Divorce Records* ☐ *Family Records* ☐ *Will & Probate*

Death Date, Location & Source _____

_____

Funeral Date, Location & Source _____

_____

Cemetery Date, Location & Source _____

_____
☐ *Biography* ☐ *Cemetery Info* ☐ *Coroner's Report* ☐ *Death Certificate* ☐ *Family Records* ☐ *Funeral Record*
☐ *Military Records* ☐ *Obituary* ☐ *Religious Death Records* ☐ *Social Security Records* ☐ *Tombstone Info*

Obituary Date _____ **Newspaper Source** _____
☐ *Biography* ☐ *Cemetery Info* ☐ *Death Certificate* ☐ *Family Records* ☐ *Funeral Record* ☐ *Newspapers*

U.S. Social Security Death Record – # and Application State _____
Last Check Address _____
☐ *Biographical Sources* ☐ *Death Certificate* ☐ *Family Records* ☐ *Obituary* ☐ *Social Security Records*

Biography Details & Source _____

_____

_____
☐ *Biography* ☐ *Business Records* ☐ *Census* ☐ *Death Certificate* ☐ *Directories* ☐ *Newspapers* ☐ *Obituary*

U.S. Federal Census Location(s) & Source _____
☐ *Biographical Sources* ☐ *Census Records* ☐ *Death Certificate* ☐ *Directories* ☐ *Newspapers* ☐ *Obituary*
Year _____ **Details:** _____
Year _____ **Details:** _____
Year _____ **Details:** _____
Year _____ **Details:** _____
Year _____ **Details:** _____
Year _____ **Details:** _____
Year _____ **Details:** _____
Year _____ **Details:** _____

© 2017, Marsha Peterson-Maass

Fundamentals of Genealogy®: Basics for Everyone

Second edition, part of the *Fundamentals of Genealogy*® textbook series

---

Ancestral Profile for (Name) _____ **Page 2**

Education & Source _____

Education & Source _____

Education & Source _____

☐ *Biographical Sources* ☐ *Business Records* ☐ *Census* ☐ *Directories* ☐ *Newspapers* ☐ *Obituary*

Place of Worship & Source _____

_____

☐ *Biographical Sources* ☐ *Newspapers* ☐ *Obituary* ☐ *Religious Records* ☐ *Vital Records*

Occupation, Employer & Source _____

_____

_____

☐ *Biographical Sources* ☐ *Business Records* ☐ *Death Certificate* ☐ *Directory Records* ☐ *Newspapers*
☐ *Obituary* ☐ *Religious Records* ☐ *Social Security Records* ☐ *Tax Records* ☐ *Tombstone Inscription*

Tax and Voter Records & Source _____

_____

☐ *Biographical Sources* ☐ *Census Records* ☐ *Death Certificate* ☐ *Tax Records* ☐ *Voter Records*

Medical Details & Source _____

_____

_____

☐ *Biographical Sources* ☐ *Death Certificate* ☐ *Family Records* ☐ *Medical Records* ☐ *Military Files*

Home Address, Dates & Source _____

  Land Ownership & Source _____

Home Address, Dates & Source _____

  Land Ownership & Source _____

Home Address, Dates & Source _____

  Land Ownership & Source _____

☐ *Biography* ☐ *Business* ☐ *Cemetery* ☐ *Census* ☐ *Educational* ☐ *Family Records* ☐ *Land Records*
☐ *Military Records* ☐ *Obituary* ☐ *Social Security Records* ☐ *Tax Records* ☐ *Vital Records*

Will/Probate & Source _____

_____

☐ *Biographical Sources* ☐ *Death Certificate* ☐ *Family Records* ☐ *Social Security Records* ☐ *Will & Probate*

U.S. Military Service & Source _____

Company, Rank, Dates _____

☐ *Biographical Sources* ☐ *Census* ☐ *Death Certificate* ☐ *Family Records* ☐ *Funeral Records* ☐ *Military
Personnel & Pension Records* ☐ *Obituary* ☐ *Social Security Records* ☐ *Tombstone Inscription*

Embarkation Date, Location & Source _____

Immigration Arrival Date, Location & Source _____

☐ *Biographical Sources* ☐ *Census Records* ☐ *Family Records* ☐ *Immigration Records* ☐ *Naturalization
Records* ☐ *Newspapers* ☐ *Obituary* ☐ *Vital Records*

Naturalization Date, Location & Source _____

☐ *Biographical Sources* ☐ *Census Records* ☐ *Family Records* ☐ *Naturalization Records* ☐ *Obituary*

Genealogy Vocabulary Terms & Concepts . . .

Clues . . . Clues are unanalyzed information. Clues become Facts after they go thru **"Evidence Evaluation & Weighing To Substantiate Proof Process."**

Collateral Relatives . . . All relatives who are not Direct Ancestors.

Conclusion . . . A result based on Facts summing up a statement of opinion.

Direct Ancestor . . . Only those ancestors who contributed to your genetic makeup; your parents, their parents, their parents, etc.

Evidence . . . Weighed information possessing reliability, credibility and relevance.

Facts . . . Evidence possessing truth (through the analysis process above).

Genealogy . . . The pursuit of finding one's ancestry. Gathering the many pieces of your ancestors' lives through documentation they left behind, putting those pieces together, and thus constructing a picture of their life experiences. Genealogy includes the science of credible research, networking, documentation, etc. It affords its adherents memberships into lineage societies, compiled family stories and lineages, family websites, new cousins and friendships, etc.

Index . . . A sequential arrangement of material, like an alpha list of names.

Information . . . Knowledge that must be put thru an analytical weighing process.

Lineage (also known as "family tree" and "pedigree") . . . Your provable descendancy from Direct Ancestors. Also known as your blood line.

Location . . . Is the geographic place where your ancestors' events occurred and where records were created. Determine the location name then and now.

Maternal . . . Pertaining to the mother's lineage or mother's side of the family.

Matrilineal (or "the mothers" line) . . . Only one line of ascent for the Subject's mother, her mother, her mother, etc., back to Mitochondrial Eve.

Paternal . . . Pertaining to the father's lineage or father's side of the family.

Patrilineal (or "the fathers" line) . . . Only one line of ascent for the Subject's father, his father, his father, etc., ascending back to Y-Adam.

Progeny . . . All of someone's offspring or bloodline throughout the generations.

Proof . . . Final part of the **"Evidence Evaluation & Weighing To Substantiate Proof Process"** by which we reach a convincing conclusion.

Proof of Pedigree . . . Today's genealogical Standard of Proof is "proof by clear and convincing evidence" and "valuing sources based on their analyzed weight."

Record Storage Facility Types (U.S.) . . . Although there are countless locations, there are four commonly-known U.S. types: 1) **Archive . . .** A building that houses public records, possibly government records, and/or other historic documents; 2) **Repository . . .** A building, possibly a warehouse, where things are kept, including records of all types; 3) **Library . . .** A place, possibly a building of its own, that houses books and other materials specifically for reading, study, reference and learning; 4) **Facility . . .** any of the proceeding.

Source . . . The entity that supplied the information, like a document from a credible institution or person.

Vital Records . . . The four record types considered to be Vital Records: 1) Birth records; 2) Marriage records; 3) Divorce records; and 4) Death records.

Genealogical Precepts ("The Standards" of Accredited Methods) . . .

- Research back one generation at a time, proving parental relationship before moving back another generation.
- Never, ever assume. Analyze your findings without ever making assumptions.
- Always try to obtain the original document or as close a copy as possible.
- Consider all unanalyzed information to be "Clues." Only after you have analyzed a Body of Information can you consider it to be "Facts."
- Accumulate a Body of Information so you can analyze the quality of each piece instead of determining truth through quantity or convenience.
- Family lore usually contains at least a grain of truth.
- Expect conflicting information. A Body of Information will typically include some accurate and some inaccurate info. Put all of the pieces thru **"Evidence Evaluation & Weighing To Substantiate Proof Process"** and use the strongest quality of evidence instead of the greatest quantity.
- Cite the source including as much detail as possible - use dates, website URL addresses, standard citation formatting, facilities where found, etc.
- Avoid genealogy scams by checking anything that smells fishy against CyndisList's "Myths, Hoaxes & Scams" at www.cyndislist.com/myths.
- Trying spelling variations of names can be key to finding "Hidden Records." Learn to check every possible name spelling when researching.
- Expect to be shocked since we people do very human things. When finding shocking info, look at it objectively without judgment and try to be gentle in sharing it with sensitive relatives.
- Be willing to share your research since you're likely not your ancestor's only descendent. Know your sharing limits and boundaries.
- Find ways to share your accurate research with others . . . *see the* **"Networking"** *and* **"Presentation"** *sections.*
- Protect the privacy of the living by not disclosing any of their info.
- Use recording standards especially for names, dates and places . . . *see the* **Fundamentals of Genealogy® Recording Style Sheet**.
- You must research at both onsite facilities and online sources for accurate, thorough "exhaustive search" results.
- To paint a complete picture of your ancestor's life, understand the historic world and local events that impacted their life.
- It's an Urban Legend that everyone's ancestors immigrated to the U.S. thru Ellis Island. Remember that Ellis Island operated between 1892-1950's, so if your ancestors arrived in the U.S. before 1892, they may have come thru the Port of Castle Garden.

Basic Genealogy Trees, Charts and Forms . . .

→ *Find forms at FamilySearch Wiki* https://family search.org/wiki/en/Genealogy_Research_Forms
→ *Create these forms with genealogical software programs (page 81).*
→ *To learn how to fill in your family tree (page 79-80).*

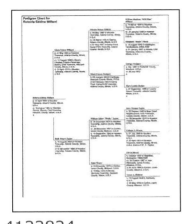

❦ **Pedigree Chart** *(at right)*–The standard form for Direct Ancestors showing generations of ascent from a subject individual. Find a lovely, free, interactive Family Tree Pedigree chart at ThoughtCo https://www.thoughtco.com/free-family-tree-charts-4122824

❦ **Family Group Sheet**-The standard one-page summary of family members' Vital Events info. Find it at the FamilySearch Wiki link above.

❦ **Genealogy Report: Register Style** *(at right)*–A report format for numbering descendants developed by NEHGS. Find a simple explanation at https://www.thoughtco.com/register-numbering-system-1420745

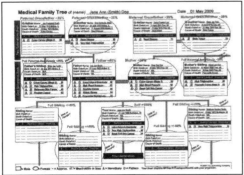

❦ **Ahnentafel Report**–A report format with each direct ancestor's vital events written on a single line beginning with their fixed number (in a numbering system related to the Subject's descent).

❦ **Descendent Family Tree**–A chart format showing a subject progenitor in a box at the top and their descendants in boxes below (ordered per generation horizontally) with lines drawn to define the parental and marital relationships.

❦ **Medical Family Tree Chart** *(at right)*–An hourglass chart displaying a family's health history per person with a subject individual at the chart's center (ancestors above, progeny below). *(pp 13-20)*

Medical Predisposition Results Sheet *(at left)*–A form for displaying a family's health history per medical condition including each family member's relationship to the subject individual, symptoms and age of disease onset. *(pages 13-22)*

Kinship Calculation Chart . . .

Bring this chart to a family reunion and use the 3 Steps below to learn your recognized kinship title with another relative!

- **"MRCA"**--the Most Recent Common Ancestor from whom people descend.
- **"Removed"**--each "removal" means a generation apart.
- **"Cousin"**--First Cousins share a grandparent MRCA; Second Cousins share a great-grandparent MRCA, etc.

Step 1–Determine the ancestor you both most recently descend from and place them in the cell titled, "Most Recent Common Ancestor" (**MRCA**).
Step 2–For yourself, find your relationship to the MRCA by looking **down the rows** and remember your Row #. *(If you are your "MRCA's Grandchild" that title is in Row 3.)* For your relative, find their relationship to the MRCA by looking **across the columns** and remember their Column #. *(If they are the "MRCA's Great-Grandchild," that title is in Column 4.)*
Step 3–Find the Kinship Title where your Row # intersects their Column #. *(Since Row 3 intersects Column 4, you are First Cousins Once Removed.)*

	Column 1	Column 2	Column 3	Column 4	Column 5	Column 6	Column 7
Row 1	**Most Recent Common Ancestor** ("MRCA")	*MRCA*'s Child	*MRCA*'s Grandchild	*MRCA*'s Great-Grandchild	*MRCA*'s Great-Great-Grandchild	*MRCA*'s Great-Great-Great Grandchild	*MRCA*'s Great-Great-Great-Great-Grandchild
Row 2	*MRCA*'s Child	Siblings	Nephew or Niece	Grandnephew or Grandniece	Great-Grandnephew or Great-Grandniece	Great-Great Grandnephew or Great-Great-Grandniece	3-Great Grandnephew or 3-Great-Grandniece
Row 3	*MRCA*'s Grandchild	Nephew or Niece	First Cousin	First Cousin Once Removed	First Cousin Twice Removed	First Cousin Thrice Removed	First Cousin Fourth Removed
Row 4	*MRCA*'s Great-Grandchild	Grandnephew or Grandniece	First Cousin Once Removed	Second Cousin	Second Cousin Once Removed	Second Cousin Twice Removed	Second Cousin Thrice Removed
Row 5	*MRCA*'s Great-Great-Grandchild	Great-Grandnephew or Great-Grandniece	First Cousin Twice Removed	Second Cousin Once Removed	Third Cousin	Third Cousin Once Removed	Third Cousin Twice Removed
Row 6	*MRCA*'s Great-Great-Great Grandchild	Great-Great Grandnephew or Great-Great-Grandniece	First Cousin Thrice Removed	Second Cousin Twice Removed	Third Cousin Once Removed	Fourth Cousin	Fourth Cousin Once Removed
Row 7	*MRCA*'s Great-Great-Great-Great-Grandchild	3-Great Grandnephew or 3-Great-Grandniece	First Cousin Fourth Removed	Second Cousin Thrice Removed	Third Cousin Twice Removed	Fourth Cousin Once Removed	Fifth Cousin

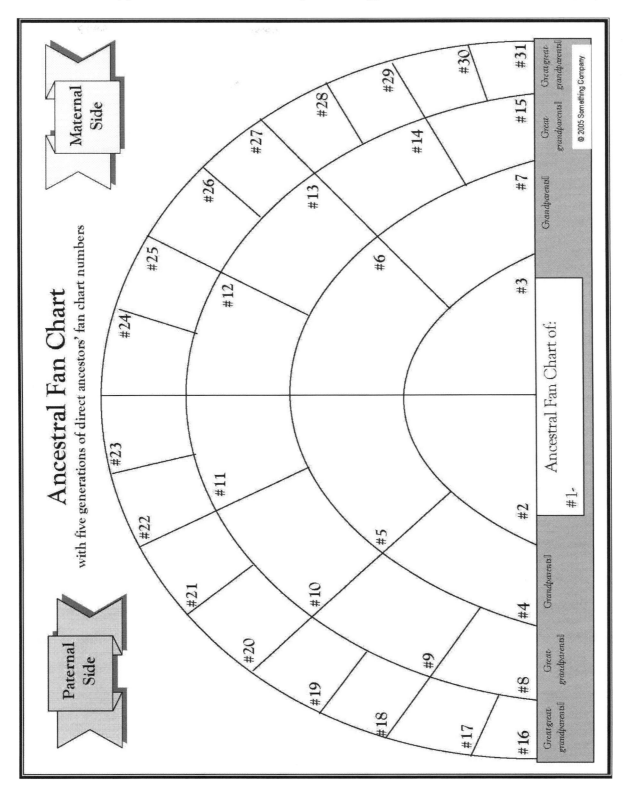

Ancestral Fan Chart

with five generations of direct ancestors' fan chart numbers

Maternal Side

Paternal Side

Ancestral Fan Chart of:

#1-

Great-great-grandparents

Great-grandparents

Grandparents

#2 #3 #4 #5 #6 #7

#8 #9 #10 #11 #12 #13 #14 #15

#16 #17 #18 #19 #20 #21 #22 #23 #24 #25 #26 #27 #28 #29 #30 #31

© 2005 Something Company

Ancestral Fan Chart . . . *is a one-page, five-generation lineage display of your Direct Ancestors with each generation representing a row of the fan. Ancestral Fan Charts usually only display full name at birth.*

🌿 You are the **subject** (Box #1) and first generation.

🌿 Your parents (Father=Box #2, Mother=Box #3) are second generation.

- Your Direct Ancestors are displayed in **PAIRS** with consecutive numbers. And since we each descend from a Father and a Mother, each ascendant generation has twice as many people as the descendant one.
- **Fathers** are listed in the left box (of each pair) having even numbers.
- **Mothers** are listed in the right box having odd numbers. Women are also listed by their maiden name (instead of married surname).
  - For example, your Paternal Grandfather would be listed in Box #4, Paternal Grandmother in Box #5, Maternal Grandfather in Box #6, and Maternal Grandmother in Box #7.

🌿 Understanding the **Ancestral Fan Chart's numbering system**:

- Each Father's number is exactly **DOUBLE** the number of his Child. To find any Father's number, take **a Child's number** and multiply by **2**.
  - For example, to find your Mother's Father (your Maternal Grandfather), take your **Mother's number (#3)** and multiply by **2**:

    #### #3 x 2 = #6 is your **Maternal Grandfather**

- Each Mother's number is exactly **ONE NUMBER HIGHER** than the Father in her PAIR. So to find any Mother's number, take **a Child's number**, multiply by **2**, then add **1**.
  - For example, to find your Mother's Mother (your Maternal Grandmother), take your **Mother's number (#3)**, multiply by **2**, then add **1**:

    #### #3 x 2 = #6 + 1 = #7 is your **Maternal Grandmother**

Ancestral Fan Chart Vocabulary

🌿 **Direct Ancestor** . . . Only those ancestors who contributed to your genetic makeup; your parents, grandparents, great-grandparents, etc.

🌿 **Paternal** . . . Pertaining to the **Father's SIDE** of the family.

🌿 **Maternal** . . . Pertaining to the **Mother's SIDE** of the family.

🌿 **Grandparent** . . . Two generations back from the Subject Individual.

🌿 **Great-Grandparent** . . . Three generations back from the Subject Individual. Also written as "gr-grandparent," "gr-gparent" or "gr-grandp."

🌿 **Great-Great-Grandparent** . . . Four generations back from the Subject Individual. Also written as "gr-gr-grandparent," "gr-gr-gparent" or "2-gr-grandparent" or "2-gr-grandp."

Summary of Today's DNA Commercial Tests . . .

Genetic Genealogy is becoming a standard genealogical practice! You must use DNA test results along with comparing accurate database cousin lineages.

❧ Three current **leading U.S.-based commercial testing companies**:
  - **FamilyTreeDNA** https://www.familytreedna.com/ *(all 3 DNA tests)*
  - **AncestryDNA** https://www.ancestry.com/dna/ *(only atDNA tests)*
  - **23andMe** https://www.23andme.com/ *(only atDNA + Medical results)*

❧ Three current **commercially-available types of DNA tests**:
  - **atDNA** chromosome test–ancestors 6-8 generations back *(all 3 DNA tests)*
  - **Y-DNA** male chromosome test – trace patrilineal line *(all 3 DNA tests)*
  - **mtDNA** mitochondrial test – trace matrilineal line *(all 3 DNA tests)*

❧ Suggestions for what to do with commercial DNA test results:
  - Join a free Project https://www.familytreedna.com/projects.aspx at FamilyTreeDNA. You can also transfer "raw data" from another company https://www.familytreedna.com/autosomal-transfer.
  - Search the company's website for how to download your "raw data" in a digital file. Save this file with your other important family papers.
  - Upload your DNA "raw data" digital file to www.GEDmatch.com.

❧ A few recommended **Facebook Groups for DNA** offering hands-on help and discussions on many DNA-related topics:
  - **Ancestry-GEDmatch-FTDNA-23andMe** https://www.facebook.com/groups/AncestryGEDmatchFTDNA23andMeGenealogyDNA/
  - **DNA Detectives** https://www.facebook.com/groups/DNADetectives/
  - **DNA4Genealogy** https://www.facebook.com/groups/dna4genealogy/
  - **DNA Newbies** https://www.facebook.com/groups/dnanewbie/
  - Find each Commercial DNA Testing Company's Facebook page.

❧ For **Adoption Research + DNA**:
  - Fundamental's U.S. Adoptions Pinterest Board https://www.pinterest.com/fgenealogy/adoption-pins-for-us-adoptee-research/
  - Currently, people are having success creating "Mirror Family Trees" in AncestryDNA®. Search YouTube for video tutorials.
  - **DNA Detectives** https://www.facebook.com/groups/DNADetectives/

Summary Of Medical Family Tree And Predisposition Results Sheet. . .

Most genealogists agree that creating a Medical Family Tree is one of the most important things they can do. Here are a few excerpts from the 2010 version of the **Fundamentals of Genealogy®: Medical Family Tree Workbook.**

There are three parts to a complete Medical Family Tree:
1) Family Records (research + answering questions).
2) A Medical Family Tree Chart listing each Health Relative's inheritable disorders + age of disease onset.
3) A Predisposition Results Sheet listing the same by disorder.

Part One---Family Records

🍂 The ultimate goal is to discuss the implications of your **accurate** Medical Family Tree and Predisposition Results Sheet with your physician or genetic counselor, understanding what "predispositions" mean (that if your close Health Relative had/has an inheritable medical condition that you have **a greater risk** than the general public of inheriting it, but that **doesn't** mean that you will **undoubtedly** manifest this condition, you're again only at a greater risk than the general public).

🍂 Genealogists already possess many **family health records**, like the Medical Cause of Death on a present-day Death Certificate.

🍂 Because you share such a large percentage of your genes with your Health Relatives, you want to identify who they are and gather their health information.

Your Primary Health Relatives (also called First Degree Health Relatives)
Those Health Relatives who share exactly 50% or an average of 50% of your genes.*

These Health Relatives in three consecutive generations share the largest percentage of common genes and therefore share the greatest chance of the same inherited medical conditions as you.
Your Parents and **Your Children** share exactly 50% of your genes (*see why in the "Basic Biology" section on page 8*).
Your Full Siblings share +/- 50% of your genes (either exactly or MORE or less than 50%).* (Which is why it's imperative to gather full sibling inform

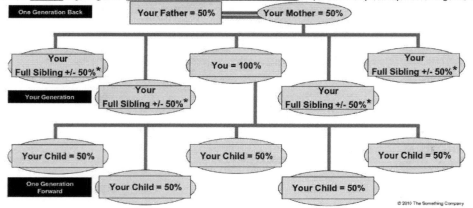

Part Two---How to fill in the Medical Family Tree Chart ("MFTC")

🍂 Review the examples of the completed MFTC and fill in the blank pages.

🍂 Gather information for at least three consecutive generations of Health Relatives (including your own generation) to determine whether there are any multi-generational patterns of disease inheritance.

🍂 Enter each Health Relative's info making sure to include Age of Disease Onset (only a Medical Family Tree gives Age of Disease Onset, not DNA currently).

Part Three---How to fill in the Predisposition Results Sheet ("PRS")

🍂 Review the examples of the completed PRS and fill in the blank page.

🍂 Take the gathered info and list all manifesting Health Relatives according to each medical condition to see patterns in symptoms + Age of Disease Onset.

🍂 Discuss the implications of this PRS with a physician or genetic counselor.

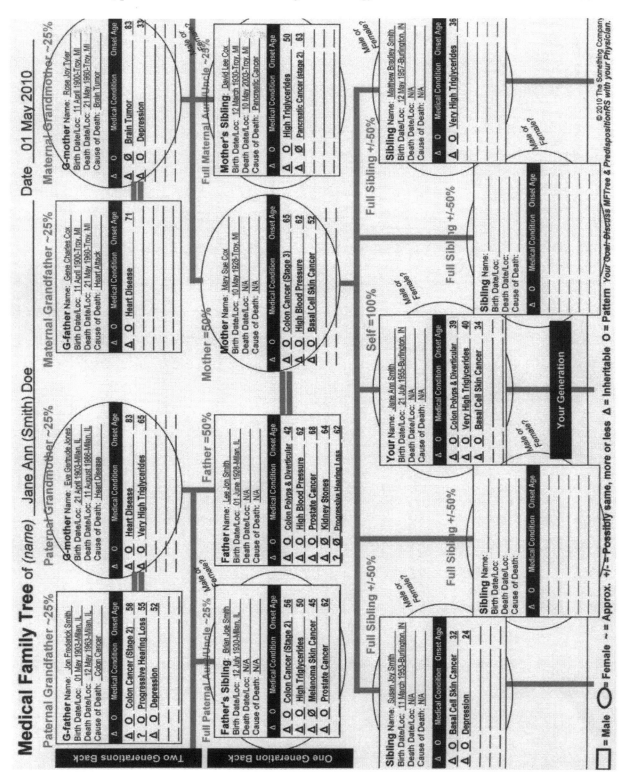

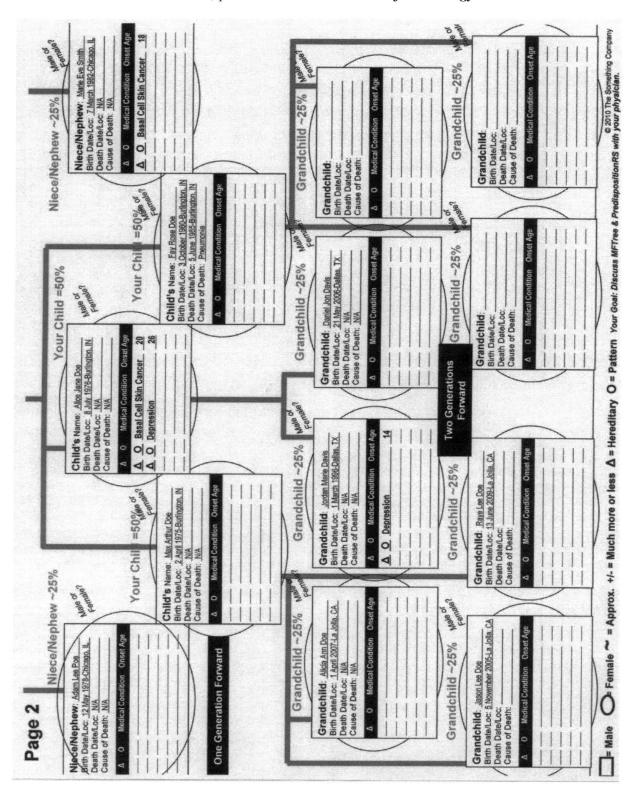

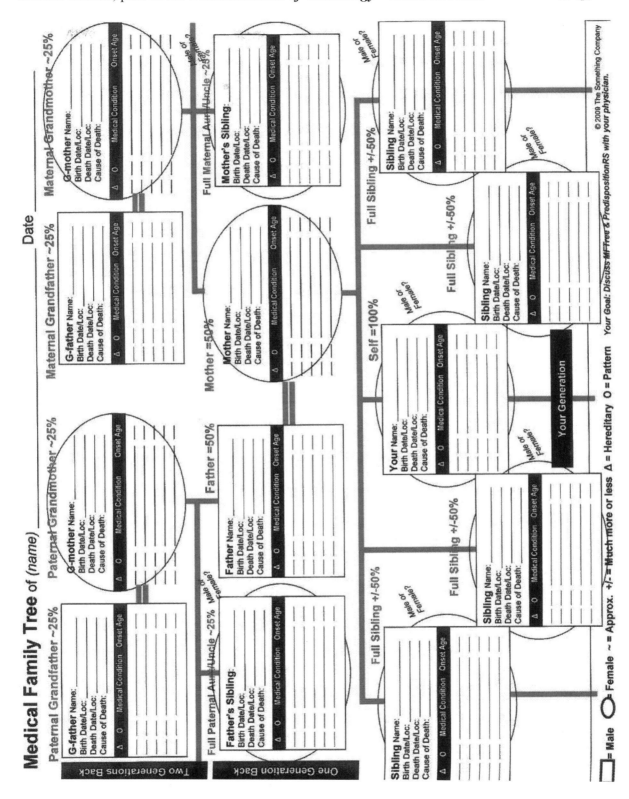

Page 2

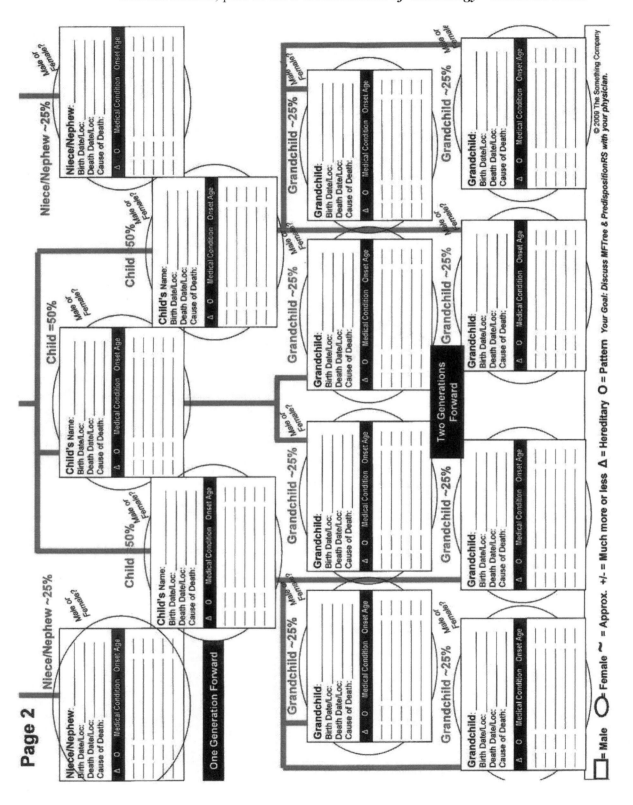

© 2009 The Something Company

Your Goal: Discuss MFTree & PredispositionRS with your physician.

□ = Male   ○ = Female   ~ = Approx.   +/- = Much more or less   Δ = Hereditary   O = Pattern

Medical Family Tree Predisposition Results Sheet — Page 1

Your Name: _Jane Ann (Smith) Doe_   [FEMALE]   Date: _01 May 2010_

Your Birth Date: _21 July 1955_   Your Birth Location: _Burlington, Cole County, Indiana, U.S.A._

Current Address: 789 Home Drive, Burlington, Cole County, Indiana, U.S.A.

See Appendix D (or an authoritative medical source) to determine whether this medical condition is hereditary. See pages 32-33 to name the type of pattern.

List Hereditary Medical Condition Pattern #1 here→ *Colon Polypsis and/or Colon Cancer*

Type of Pattern #1 here→ *Consecutive Multi-Gen. Paternal and Consecutive Bi-Gen. Maternal Pattern*

Name of each relative with this condition	Age of Onset	Relationship %	Family Line
1. Self – Jane (Smith) Doe – Colon Polypsis	Age 39	100% self	Sib/Pat/Mat/Prog
2. Mother – Mary Susan (Cox) Smith – Colon Cancer	Age 65 = Stage 3 Survivor	50% primary HR	Maternal
3. Father – Lee Jon Smith – Colon Polypsis & Spinal Cysts	Age 42	50% primary HR	Paternal
4. Paternal G-father – Jon Frederick Smith – Colon Cancer	Age 58 = Cause of Death	~25% secondary HR	Paternal
5. Paternal Uncle – Brian Joe Smith – Colon Cancer	Age 56 = Stage 2 Survivor	~25% secondary HR	Paternal
6. Paternal Aunt – Sarah (Smith) Brown – Colon Polypsis	Age 50	~25% secondary HR	Paternal

Some possible Symptoms (see Appendix D or an authoritative medical source)

Possible Symptoms: • Rectal bleeding or blood in the stool • Change in bowel movements including constipation or diarrhea • Abdominal pain with bowel movement • Unexplained weight loss, weakness and fatigue.

Some possible Prevention and Treatment options (see Appendix D or an authoritative medical source)

Possible Prevention: • If in your MFTree, early screening is mandatory • Regular screening = colonoscopy to find and remove polyps.
Possible Treatment: • After colon polyp removal, polyp malignancy is determined. If no malignancy, no further treatment is needed. If malignant, doctor will pursue cancer treatment (possibly including surgery) appropriate to the location and stage of cancer development.

See Appendix D (or an authoritative medical source) to determine whether this medical condition is hereditary. See pages 32-33 to name the type of pattern.

List Hereditary Medical Condition Pattern #2 here→ *Heart Disease, High Blood Pressure, etc.*

Type of Pattern #2 here→ *Consecutive Bi-Generational Dual-Sided Pattern*

Name of each relative with this condition	Age of Onset	Relationship %	Family Line
1. Mother – Mary Susan (Cox) Smith – High Blood Pressure	Age 62	50% primary HR	Maternal
2. Father – Lee Jon Smith – High Blood Pressure	Age 62	50% primary HR	Paternal
3. Paternal G-mother – Eve (Jones) Smith – Heart Disease	Age 83 = Cause of Death	~25% secondary HR	Paternal
4. Paternal Aunt – Sarah (Smith) Brown – High Blood Pres.	Age 56	~25% secondary HR	Paternal
5. Maternal G-father – Gene C. Cox – Heart Attack/Disease	Age 71 = Cause of Death	~25% secondary HR	Maternal

Some possible Symptoms (see Appendix D or an authoritative medical source)

Possible Symptoms: • Often caused by arteriosclerosis • Also caused by congenital heart, heart valve and heart muscle diseases • High cholesterol levels (including elevated blood glucose and triglycerides) • High blood pressure • Obesity (abdominal obesity in women).

Some possible Prevention and Treatment options (see Appendix D or an authoritative medical source)

Possible Prevention: • Daily aspirin treatment per your physician • Manage conditions that may be contributing factors, like high cholesterol, high blood pressure and diabetes. Possible Treatment: • Healthy Lifestyle = No smoking, stay active, maintain a healthy weight • Doctor prescribed medications.

See Appendix D (or an authoritative medical source) to determine whether this medical condition is hereditary. See pages 32-33 to name the type of pattern.

List Hereditary Medical Condition Pattern #3 here→ *High Triglycerides (bad cholesterol)*

Type of Pattern #3 here→ *Consecutive Multi-Gen. Paternal and Consecutive Bi-Gen. Maternal Pattern*

Name of each relative with this condition	Age of Onset	Relationship %	Family Line
1. Self – Jane (Smith) Doe – Very High Triglycerides	Age 40	100% self	Sib/Pat/Mat/Prog
2. Brother – Matthew Smith – Very High Triglycerides	Age 36	+/- 50% primary HR	Sib/Pat/Mat
3. Paternal G-mother – Eve (Jones) Smith – Very High Trigl	about Age 65	~25% secondary HR	Paternal
4. Paternal Uncle – Brian Smith – High Triglycerides	Age 50	~25% secondary HR	Paternal
5. Maternal Uncle – David Lee Cox – High Triglycerides	about Age 50	~25% secondary HR	Maternal

Some possible Symptoms (see Appendix D or an authoritative medical source)

Possible Symptoms: • There are no symptoms of high blood cholesterol; a lipid panel blood test can detect its presence.

Some possible Prevention and Treatment options (see Appendix D or an authoritative medical source)

Possible Treatment: • Lifestyle changes = healthy diet, regular exercise and avoid smoking • Depending on factors = medication(s) like statins, resins, cholesterol absorption inhibitors.

© 2010, The Something Company

Medical Family Tree Predisposition Results Sheet — Page 1

Your Name: _____ Date: _____

Your Birth Date: _____ Your Birth Location: _____

Current Address: _____

See Appendix D (or an authoritative medical source) to determine whether this medical condition is hereditary. See pages 32-33 to name the type of pattern.

List Hereditary Medical Condition Pattern #1 here→

Type of Pattern #1 here→

Name of each relative with this condition	Age of Onset	Relationship %	Family Line
1.			
2.			
3.			
4.			
5.			

Some possible Symptoms (see Appendix D or an authoritative medical source)

Some possible Prevention and Treatment options (see Appendix D or an authoritative medical source)

See Appendix D (or an authoritative medical source) to determine whether this medical condition is hereditary. See pages 32-33 to name the type of pattern.

List Hereditary Medical Condition Pattern #2 here→

Type of Pattern #2 here→

Name of each relative with this condition	Age of Onset	Relationship %	Family Line
1.			
2.			
3.			
4.			
5.			

Some possible Symptoms (see Appendix D or an authoritative medical source)

Some possible Prevention and Treatment options (see Appendix D or an authoritative medical source)

See Appendix D (or an authoritative medical source) to determine whether this medical condition is hereditary. See pages 32-33 to name the type of pattern.

List Hereditary Medical Condition Pattern #3 here→

Type of Pattern #3 here→

Name of each relative with this condition	Age of Onset	Relationship %	Family Line
1.			
2.			
3.			
4.			
5.			

Some possible Symptoms (see Appendix D or an authoritative medical source)

Some possible Prevention and Treatment options (see Appendix D or an authoritative medical source)

Fundamentals of Genealogy®: Basics for Everyone

Second edition, part of the *Fundamentals of Genealogy®* textbook series

How to Find U.S. Public & Private Sources
Family Sources (including How To Interview Family) . . .

Gather information from the family sources below since they might be some of the best clues to your ancestors. Make sure to also interview relatives (the elderly first) and use the quick checklist below to maximize your results!

Anniversary records	Divorce records	Licenses	Pension records
Baby books + records	Family Reunion records	Marriage records	Photo albums
Bible records	Family Traditions	Medical records	Religious records
Birth certificates + records	Funeral records	Memorabilia	Scrapbooks
Business records	Heirlooms	Military records	School records
Club & Org. records	Insurance records	Naturalization records	Tax records
Death records	Land records	Newspaper clippings	Wedding albums
Diaries	Letters, etc.	Passport records	Wills/Probate

- Record the **family lore** for both your paternal and maternal lines. Include the source of this information. Date it. Revisit it in a few years and see the difference your genealogical research has made!
- **Interview** your relative by telling them that that there are no "rights or wrongs" in collecting their info, you simply want to know what they know. Since you're the researcher, after retrieving their info, you'll research to verify the facts. Use the checklist below:

	Before all else = Define your needs! Should you compile background?
	Before = Have you scheduled a date and time for this interview?
	Before = Have you given the interviewee the "Family Sources" list above?
	Before = Have you given the interviewee photos to jog their memory?
	Before = Have you given the interviewee any questions beforehand?
	→ *What questions will answer your needs? It's important to get locations.*
	→ *Can interviewee give a source for how they know each piece of info?*
	→ *Speculation and guesses are okay if they are clearly identified as such.*
	→ **Question:** Your Vital Events info? (Birth, Marriage, Divorce)
	→ **Question**: Identify your parents and happiest memories of them?
	→ **Question**: What was a value your parents taught you?
	→ **Question**: Repeat the last two questions for your grandparents?
	→ **Question**: Tell of your childhood. Happy? Active? School? Friends?
	→ **Question**: How did you meet your spouse? First date? Memories?
	→ **Question**: What jobs/career have you had? Any relatives have the same?
	→ **Question**: Do you have a favorite saying or advice for a happy life?
	→ **Question**: Which relatives do you remember + can you share memories?
	→ **Question**: What are family traditions and your memories of them?
	→ **Question**: What is the family lore? Any famous or notorious relatives?
	→ **Question**: What would you like future generations to know of the family?
	After = Can you record this interview to preserve it?
	After = Transcribe the interview afterward.

How to Find U.S. Public & Private Sources

U.S. National, State And Local Sources[1] . . .

As genealogists we try to find the records our ancestors left behind in the places where they lived. Familiarizing yourself with important U.S. genealogical institutions will help you understand what sources are available and how to obtain the records.

Important U.S. National & State Genealogical Libraries, Repositories And Archives *(that hold genealogical records)*

🌺 *Find more recommendations in the "**Library**" section of **Fundamentals of Genealogy®: The Most Helpful Tools You've Never Used**.*

🌺 **Allen County Public Library** www.acpl.lib.in.us/ in Fort Wayne, Indiana has a premier periodical collection (it maintains PERSI), local histories, databases, genealogies, military, directories, passenger lists, etc.
- **ACPL Genealogy Center** http://www.genealogycenter.org/
  - **Databases** www.genealogycenter.org/Databases.aspx
  - **Historical Genealogy Quick-Search Services** www.genealogycenter .org/docs/default-source/resources/quicksearchrequest.pdf?sfvrsn=2
  - **Pathfinder "State and Subject Snapshots"** www.genealogycenter.org/Pathfinders/Snapshots.aspx
  - **State Resources** www.genealogycenter.info/otherstates/

🌺 **BYU Family History Library** https://sites.lib.byu.edu/familyhistory/ has online tools including Lab Resources and lists of genealogical links for FHC Subjects, Digital State Archives, Records, Reference, Maps, etc.
- **Digital State Archives** https://sites.lib.byu.edu/familyhistory/digital-archives/
- **Records** https://sites.lib.byu.edu/familyhistory/records/
- **Reference** https://sites.lib.byu.edu/familyhistory/reference/

🌺 **Dallas Public Library's Genealogy Collection (J. Erik Jonsson Central Library)** http://dallaslibrary2.org/genealogy/index.php has online databases plus book and microfilm of originals for some state and county marriage, probate, deed and tax abstracts.

🌺 **Daughters of the American Revolution** www.dar.org/ in Washington, D.C. specializes in early American records with "many thousands of volumes of genealogical compilations, record abstracts . . . book collection exceeds 225,000 volumes," and also offers online databases, special collections and research guides.

---

[1] National Genealogical Society's "**Guidelines for Using Records Repositories and Libraries**" http://www.ngsgenealogy.org/cs/ngs_guidelines

---

- **The Americana Collection** www.dar.org/archives . . . "focus of the collection is on Colonial America, the Revolutionary War Era, and the early Republic, but the breadth of the collection spans five centuries."

🌿 **Family History Library** https://familysearch.org/locations/saltlakecity-library "in Salt Lake City has about 500 computers, +3M microforms, 5,000 periodicals, +300,000 books, and microfilm/digitized records including vital, immigration, ethnic, military, and more."

- **FamilySearch Online Catalog (of the Family History Library)** https://familysearch.org/catalog/search "Search the catalog of genealogical materials (including books, online materials, microfilm, microfiche, and publications) made available by FamilySearch. Many items can be loaned to local family history centers around the world."
- **Family History Centers** https://familysearch.org/locations/ are +4500 local library branches located worldwide (often at Mormon churches).

🌿 **Library of Congress ("LOC")** www.loc.gov/rr/genealogy/ the Washington, D.C. Local History and Genealogy Reading Room includes genealogies, local histories, manuscripts, microfilms, maps, newspapers, photographs, and books.

🌿 **Mid-Continent Public Library's Midwest Genealogy Center** www.mymcpl.org/genealogy in Independence, Missouri, contains +80,000 family histories, 100,000 local histories, 565,000 microfilms, 7,000 maps, newspapers and much more.

🌿 **National Archives and Records Administration ("NARA")** https://www.archives.gov has millions of original records that can be obtained thru mail, online order and microfilm sent to regional facilities.

- **NARA Online Resources for Genealogists** https://www.archives.gov/research/genealogy find Start Your Family Research, Browse Popular Topics, Events, Tools, Help NARA Transcribe Records, and much more.
  - **Access to Archival Databases** https://aad.archives.gov/aad/
  - **Charts and Forms** https://www.archives.gov/research/genealogy/charts-forms
  - **NARA's Online Catalog** https://www.archives.gov/research/catalog
  - **Online Research Tools and Aids** https://www.archives.gov/research/start/online-tools.html
- **All of NARA's Facilities including Regional Repositories** https://www.archives.gov/locations
- **Record Groups and Order Forms:**
  - **Research on Ethnic Heritage** https://www.archives.gov/research/genealogy/ethnic-heritage.html
  - **NARA Forms** https://www.archives.gov/forms

- **Genealogy Research Topics** https://www.archives.gov/research/genealogy/topics.html
- **Immigration Records** https://www.archives.gov/research/immigration and order records NATF 84 https://www.archives.gov/contact#81
- **Land Records** https://www.archives.gov/research/land and use form NATF 84 to order records https://www.archives.gov/contact#84
- **Military Records** https://www.archives.gov/research/military "How to Obtain Copies of Records" https://www.archives.gov/research/order
- **Passport Records** https://www.archives.gov/research/passport obtain copies via email at inquire@nara.gov

- **New England History Genealogical Society ("NEHGS")** https://www.americanancestors.org/index.aspx in Boston specializes in New England and New York State resources (since the 1600s) including +100M name database, online education, vital records, genealogies, journals, +200,000 books, 100,000 microfilms, and +20M manuscripts.
- **New York Public Library's Genealogy Collections ("NYPL")** https://www.nypl.org/about/divisions have American history, international genealogy and heraldry, archives and manuscripts, the Dorot Jewish collection, digitized materials, photos, and New York censuses, directories, and vital records.
- **The Newberry Library's Genealogy and Local History Collections** www.newberry.org/genealogy-and-local-history in Chicago has an outstanding array of online and book/film for most states - genealogies, local histories, city & county directories, indexes, military records, etc.
- **SAR Genealogical Research Library (Sons of the American Revolution)** https://sar.org/sar-genealogical-research-library in Louisville, Kentucky with primary focus on "the collections is the Revolutionary War era but the collection includes other materials of a genealogical nature. To date the library collection has grown to over 55,000 items and includes family histories, local, county and state records and genealogy materials, and access to the online databases."
- **Sutro Library** www.library.ca.gov/calhist/genealogy.html in San Francisco specializes in genealogy and CA history with thousands of books, microforms, histories & genealogies, rare books, etc.
- *Find local repositories for governmental records below.*

How To Find U.S. National, State & <u>LOCAL</u> Genealogical <u>Repositories</u>

- Use **CyndisList** www.cyndislist.com/ to help find "all things genealogy"
  - Libraries, Archives & Museums www.cyndislist.com/libraries/lending/locality/
  - U.S. Vital Records www.cyndislist.com/us/vital/
- **FamilySearch Wiki** https://familysearch.org/wiki Search on the location.

❧ **Google** https://www.google.com use keyword searches like the location name and "vital records."

❧ **USGenWeb Project** www.usgenweb.org/ a free website where "a group of volunteers working together to provide free genealogy websites for genealogical research in every county and every state of the United States . . . organization is by county and state, and this website provides you with links to all the state genealogy websites which, in turn, provide gateways to the counties."

❧ **Vital Rec** http://vitalrec.com/ a free database that creators call "the most comprehensive resource for locating U.S. local vital records - Birth Certificates, Death Records, Divorce Decrees & Marriage Licenses."

❧ **WorldGenWeb Project** www.worldgenweb.org/ a free website of a "volunteer based organization dedicated to providing genealogical and historical records and resources for world-wide access!"

Recommended Genealogical Records/Resources <u>Database Providers</u>

❧ **Ancestry®** www.ancestry.com (subscription or use at your public library) More than 5 billion searchable names, hundreds of data collections from around the world, create your online family tree (with ability to attach digital record sources), network and Ancestry® Wiki has many tools.

 • **Support Center** https://support.ancestry.com/s/ "Search & Records" offers articles to Getting Started, Beyond the Basics, Census, Immigration, Military, Ethnic Resources & Research, etc.

 • **U.S. State Research Guides** in the Support Center (above - click "Search & Records," then in the search box type "U.S. State Research Guides"), "include state historical backgrounds, information about census and vital records, highlighted collections for the state on Ancestry, and links to resources beyond Ancestry."

 • **CyndisList** "Ancestry.com-The Basics" www.cyndislist.com/ancestry/

❧ **CyndisList** "Database" www.cyndislist.com/cyndislistsearch/?q=database

❧ **FamilySearch** https://familysearch.org and its online searchable database record collections and indexes is part of the largest genealogy organization in the world. And it's free. Create your online family tree (with ability to attach digital record sources), read digitized books, network, FamilySearch Wiki is many genealogists "Go To" and more.

 • **FamilySearch Books** https://familysearch.org/search >> click "Books"-"Family History Books is a collection of more than 325,000 digitized genealogy and family history publications from the archives of some of the most important family history libraries in the world. The collection includes family histories, county and local histories, genealogy magazines and how-to books, gazetteers, and medieval histories."

- **FamilySearch's Learning Center** https://familysearch.org/learning center/home.html "Browse hundreds of online genealogy courses to help you discover your family history."
- **CyndisList** www.cyndislist.com/cyndislistsearch/?q=familysearch

- **FindAGrave** https://www.findagrave.com/ free online database to "Find the graves of ancestors, create virtual memorials" and much more.

- **Fold3** https://www.fold3.com (subscription) "millions of historical documents and photos specializing in military records and stories."

- **Google Books** https://books.google.com "Search the world's most comprehensive index of full-text books" many with genealogical content.

- **HeritageQuest** (possibly free thru your public library's online subscription) www.ancestryheritagequest.com "Includes family histories, genealogical serials, local histories, the U.S. Federal Census, 1790-1930, and primary sources in full images."

- **Internet Archive** https://archive.org/ a non-profit library with millions of free resources including digitized genealogical books.

- **MyHeritage** https://www.myheritage.com/ "Used by millions of people worldwide to help research family history, build a family tree, and add photos, historical records, and more."

- **NewspaperArchive** https://newspaperarchive.com/ "NewspaperArchive .com is the world's largest online newspaper archive. Featuring billions of articles from historical newspapers around the U.S. and the world."

- **Newspapers.com** https://www.newspapers.com/ Find nearly 5,000 "historical newspapers from across the United States and beyond."

- **PERSI** (PERiodical Source Index) a FREE searchable index, now located online at www.findmypast.com/persi , has nearly 3M genealogical journal entries for articles from +8,000 international but primarily U.S.-based national and local genealogical, historical and ethnic periodicals. It's consistently updated by the Allen County (IN) Public Library (so remember to keep checking it "periodically," sorry couldn't resist).

- **RootsWeb** http://home.rootsweb.ancestry.com/ "The oldest and largest free genealogy site now part of the Ancestry.com community."

- **Vital Rec** http://vitalrec.com/ a free database that creators call "the most comprehensive resource for locating U.S. local vital records - Birth Certificates, Death Records & Marriage Licenses."

- **World Vital Records** (possibly free thru your public library's online subscription) www.worldvitalrecords.com/wvrhome.aspx offers "Access to birth, marriage, and death records; Social Security Death Index; family trees; census records; immigration records; court, land, and probate records; military records directory lists; newspapers, family histories,

reference materials, biographies, wills, gravestone photos, ship manifests, map collections, and yearbook collections."
* **WorldCat** www.worldcat.org/ a free, searchable online index that "Connects you to 2 billion items from the collections and services of more than 10,000 libraries worldwide."

Recommended Genealogical <u>Resources Organizations</u> *(that might **not** hold original genealogical records but other important gen. resources)*
* **CyndisList** "Organizations" www.cyndislist.com/cyndislistsearch/?q=organizations
* **CyndisList** "Records" www.cyndislist.com/cyndislistsearch/?q=records
* **GeneaBloggers** www.geneabloggers.com/ find genealogy blogs.
* **U.S. National Genealogical Society ("NGS")** www.ngsgenealogy.org/ find Education, Publications & Videos, Events, Research References, links to their Social Media and much more.
  * **The NGS "Research in the States" publication series** www.ngsgenealogy.org/cs/research_in_the_states

Important U.S. Genealogical & Historical <u>Societies</u>
An often overlooked wealth of both public and private genealogical sources can be found at U.S. genealogical and historical societies. Find them here.
* **BYU Family History Library's "Libraries and Historical Societies"** https://sites.lib.byu.edu/familyhistory/libraries-historical-societies/
* **FamilySearch.org Wiki** https://familysearch.org/wiki/en/Main_Page
* **Federation of Genealogical Societies** ("FGS") http://fgs.org/
* **National Genealogical Society** ("NGS") www.ngsgenealogy.org
* **Obituary Links Page** – U.S. Gen. Societies www.obitlinkspage.com/hs/
* **YouTube** www.YouTube.com search for organizations' channels

How to Find Other U.S. <u>Organizations</u> with local record collections
You could find some really valuable information if you search locally.
* **CyndisList "Societies"** www.cyndislist.com/cyndislistsearch/?q=societies
* **Google** https://www.google.com topics + location (especially ethnic & business)
* **Local Private & Public Libraries** may hold special record collections.
* **USGenWeb** http://usgenweb.org/ search by state and county
* **Vital Rec** http://vitalrec.com/ leading to U.S. local vital records.
* **YouTube** www.YouTube.com search for genealogical topics (especially ethnic & profession) and also for geographic locations.

Recommended <u>Educational Resources</u> for your genealogical pursuits
Find a wealth of genealogical knowledge in these paper + online resources.
* **Online Articles & Guides**

- **Ancestry® Wiki** www.ancestry.com/wiki find the most popular articles on the Main Page and links to Tools, World Archives Project, Search feature, online text from *The Source* and *Redbook* and more.
  - **Ancestry® Academy** https://www.ancestry.com/academy/
  - **YouTube Channel** https://www.youtube.com/user/AncestryCom
- **Board for the Certification of Genealogists' "Skillbuilding: Your Learning Center"** www.bcgcertification.org/skillbuilders/index.html
- **BYU Family History Portal** http://familyhistory.byu.edu/
  - **BYU Family History Library** https://sites.lib.byu.edu/familyhistory/
  - **BYU Center for Family History and Genealogy** https://cfhg.byu.edu/Pages/Home.aspx
- **CyndisList** www.cyndislist.com/ search using keywords for the topic plus words like "how to," "guide" and "instruction."
- **DearMYRTLE** http://blog.dearmyrtle.com/
  - **YouTube Channel** https://www.youtube.com/user/DearMYRTLE
  - **Webinars** http://blog.dearmyrtle.com/p/geneawebinarscalendar.html
- **Eastman's Online Genealogy Newsletter** https://blog.eogn.com/
- **FamilySearch Wiki** https://familysearch.org/wiki/en/Main_Page much of this Wiki is locality-based. On the Home Page, find the Search feature, New to Genealogy, New to the Wiki?, and many Tools in the left sidebar section.
  - **FamilySearch Help Center** https://familysearch.org/ask/landing >> click "Genealogy Assistance"
  - **YouTube Channel** https://www.youtube.com/user/familysearch
- **Family Tree Magazine** www.familytreemagazine.com/ free and subscription to many online articles and tools.
- **HeritageQuest "Research Aids"** (thru your public library's online subscription) www.ancestryheritagequest.com/HQA/ResearchAids
- **(U.S.) National Archives and Records Admin.'s Resources for Genealogy ("NARA")** https://www.archives.gov/research/genealogy find Start Your Family Research, Browse Popular Topics, Events, Tools for Genealogists, Help NARA Transcribe Records and more.
- **(U.S.) National Genealogical Society ("NGS")** www.ngsgenealogy.org/ find Education, Publications & Videos, Events, Research References, links to their Social Media and much more.
  - **National Genealogical Society's Educational Courses** www.ngsgenealogy.org/cs/educational_courses
- **One-Step Webpages by Stephen P. Morse** www.stevemorse.org/ "This site contains tools for finding immigration records, census records, vital records, and for dealing with calendars, maps, foreign alphabets, and numerous other applications. Some of these tools fetch

data from other websites but do so in more versatile ways than the search tools provided on those websites."

- **RootsWeb** http://home.rootsweb.ancestry.com/ a free part of the Ancestry community where you'll find Getting Started, Search Engines & Databases, Tools and Resources and much more.
- **ThoughtCo's Genealogy** https://www.thoughtco.com/genealogy-4133308 "Start building your family tree with expert-written genealogy tutorials, database recommendations, surname meanings, search strategies, and ancestry charts."

❧ **Other Learning Opportunities for genealogical instruction**
- **NGS Learning Opportunities** (U.S. National Genealogical Society) www.ngsgenealogy.org/cs/educational_courses

❧ **Textbooks for genealogical instruction**
- Croom, Emily Ann. ***Unpuzzling Your Past: The Best-Selling Basic Guide to Genealogy.*** 3d edition. Baltimore, Maryland, U.S.A.: Genealogical Publishing Company, 2010.
- Greenwood, Val D. ***The Researcher's Guide to American Genealogy.*** 3d edition. Baltimore, Maryland, U.S.A.: Genealogical Publishing Company, 2000.
- Peterson-Maass, Marsha. ***Fundamentals of Genealogy®: Basics for Everyone.*** Lulu Publishing Company www.Lulu.com, 2017.
- Szucs, Loretto Dennis and Sandra Hargreaves Luebking. ***The Source: A Guidebook of American Genealogy.*** 3rd edition. Salt Lake City, Utah, U.S.A.: Ancestry Inc., 2006.

❧ **YouTube's video genealogical instruction** https://www.youtube.com/ search with keywords for the topic of interest. Also see these YouTube Channels from renowned genealogical organizations.
- **Ancestry®** https://www.youtube.com/user/AncestryCom
- **BYU Family History Library** https://www.youtube.com/channel/UC7hqNOQt-2AfeVEpDuc7sCA
- **DearMYRTLE** https://www.youtube.com/user/DearMYRTLE
- **FamilySearch** https://www.youtube.com/user/FamilySearch
- **Family Tree Magazine** https://www.youtube.com/user/familytreemagazine
- **NGS Genealogy** https://www.youtube.com/user/NGSGenealogy
- **US National Archives** https://www.youtube.com/user/usnationalarchives

IMPORTANT U.S. PUBLIC & PRIVATE SOURCES . . . *HOW TO FIND MORE SOURCES*

*Indepth exposition, see "**Recommended for Record Groups**" (pages 29-31), the **FamilySearch Wiki** and **FamilySearch Help Center** (page 30).*

Basic U.S. Genealogical Records Group
Birth Records . . .

U.S. Birth Records	Birth Records Locations + What To Check
Baptismal Certificate	**Family Sources** .... *page 23*
Baptismal Records-Church	• Check for Vital Records in Family Papers and Interviews with Relatives
Baptismal Records-Clerk	• Check for Bible and other Religious Records
Birth Certificate	**Important U.S. Nat'l & State Gen. Libraries, Repos. & Archives** ...*24-26*
Birth Record-Bible Record	• Check for State-level Vital Records
Birth Record-Diary/Journal	• Check for Bible and other Religious Records
Birth Record-Lineage	**How to Find LOCAL Genealogical Repositories** *26-27*
Birth Record-Military	• Check County Clerk & Courthouse for Local-level Vital Records
Birth Record-Naturalization	• Check for Local Newspaper and other public records
Birth Record-Newspaper	**Recommended Gen. Records/Resources Database Providers**......*27-29*
Birth Record-Vital Records	• Check for Family Trees, Vital Records, Military, Naturalization, etc.
Birth Registration-Civil	**Important U.S. Genealogical & Historical Societies**...........................*29*
	• Check for Local Vital Records and other record collections
	• Check for Bible and other Religious Records
	• Check for Members' Lineage and other Family Records

Description of Birth Records

Birth records are one of the four types of Vital Records. They have evolved with our country's growth, primarily in family and church records in early days, then later maintained at both the State and County governmental level. Their form and info differ greatly with the recording entity, location and time period.

❧ You'll find State privacy laws surrounding Governmental Birth Records. Check for records at both the State and County level. For early records, like most of New England, they might be found at the Town level.

❧ The date availability of Governmental Birth Records depends largely on when each State and County began requiring them.

Clues to Birth Information might be found *in Biographical information.*

Obtain Documents for Birth Records

❧ **VitalRec.com** www.vitalrec.com/ leads you to the State and Local governmental vital records repositories. Choose "Birth," then the State for

date availability and fees. Proceed to the County (to check dates and fees). Varying State privacy laws apply.
- 🌿 Check home sources for various death records.
- 🌿 Check local sources for religious records.
- 🌿 Check the Birth Records chart above. Pay special attention to the "**How to Find LOCAL Genealogical Repositories**" section (pages *26-27*).

Recommended Guides To Birth Research In General

Recommended Guides To Birth Research In Their Collection

Recommended Textbooks for Birth Research

Basic U.S. Genealogical Records Group
Business Records . . .

U.S. Business Records	Business & Employment Records Locations + What To Check
Apprenticeship Records	**Family Sources** .... *page 23*
Business Licenses	• Check for Bio Records in Family Papers and Interviews with Relatives
Employee Records	**Important U.S. Nat'l & State Gen. Libraries, Repos. & Archives** ...*24-26*
Farming Records	• Check for State-level Business & Employment Archive Records
Small Business Records	**How to Find LOCAL Genealogical Repositories** 26-27
Tax Records	• Check County Clerk & Courthouse for Local-level Business Records
	• Check for Local Newspaper and other public records
	Recommended Gen. Records/Resources Database Providers......*27-29*
	• Check for Tax Records, Union Records, Employer Records, etc.
	Important U.S. Genealogical & Historical Societies.............................29
	• Check for Local Business & Taxl Records and other record collections
	• Check for Business Licenses and Newspaper Ads & Articles
	• Check for Members' Lineage and other Family Records for clues

Description of Business Records
Find clues in your ancestors' other biographical records, then go find these business & employment records! Try to identify their job, employer, business

type, etc., to determine what business records were created about them.

Clues to Business & Employment Information might be found:
Start by checking Census Records (both Population and "Special Schedules"), City & County Directories, Passport Applications, Tax Records, Military Records, U.S. Social Security Records, Newspaper-Obits, etc.

Obtain Documents for Business & Employment Records
* Check the Business Records chart above. Pay attention to the "**How to Find LOCAL Genealogical Repositories"** section (pages *26-27*).
* If an **Employee**, even in an unusual industry:
   1 - Review **family records** for an employer's name, location & dates
   2 - Put this occupation in its **Historic Context** by putting the correct person in the correct place at the correct time.
   3 - Determine whether there's a **company archive** . . . Google and ask questions . . . check NUCMC and other local archives *(page 72)* . . . "**Recommended Genealogical Records/Resources Database Providers**" section . . . go to Social Media and ask questions ("**Networking**" section).
   4 - Search for **general industry information** to use in a biography, starting with Google and CyndisList.
* If an **Employer or Small Business Owner**:
   * Check City and County Directories, Business Licenses, Newspapers, Tax Records, etc.
* If **Farmers or Farmhands:**
   * Search the **U.S. Agricultural Censuses for 1850, 1860, 1870 and 1880**. They offer information like land location, type and value. Other information might include inventories of livestock, crops and by-products. Also look at neighbors for possible relatives and other clues.
      * Search the **U.S. Products of Industry and Manufacture Census Schedules for 1820, 1850, 1860, 1870 and 1880** that detailed a wide variety of industrial businesses. Along with the company name, there was info taken on the top four raw materials used to create the product, number of employees, etc.
   * **Farmer's Directories** --- an example is the *Prairie Farmer's Reliable Directory* searchable on Ancestry.com . . . see the "**Recommended Genealogical Records/Resources Database Providers**" section
* **Apprenticeship Records** https://familysearch.org/blog/en/apprenticeship-records-family-historians/

- ❧ **Railroad Employee Records** --- U.S., Chicago and North Western Railroad Employment Records, 1935-1970
http://search.ancestrylibrary.com/search/db.aspx?dbid=6944
- ❧ **Pullman Car Works** --- SSGHS has a closed collection and offer FREE "employee file" lookup, then $15 file if found www.ssghs.org/pullman.htm
- ❧ **AFL-CIO's list of Workers' Memorials** (listed by state)
www.aflcio.org/Issues/Job-Safety/WorkersMemorialDay/A-Collection-of-Workers-Memorials
- ❧ ***Dictionary of Ancient Occupations & Trades, Ranks, Offices & Title***
http://freepages.genealogy.rootsweb.ancestry.com/~dav4is/Sources/Occupations.html

Recommended Guides To Business Research In General

Recommended Guides To Business Research In Their Collection

Recommended Textbooks for Business Research

Basic U.S. Genealogical Records Group
Cemetery Records . . .

Cemetery Records	Cemetery Records Locations + What To Check
Bible Records	**Family Sources** .... *page 23*
Burial Permits, Registers and other records	• Check for Death Records in Family Papers and Interviews with Relatives • Check for Bible and other Religious Records
Cemetery Deed, Plot Register and Records, Association Records	**How to Find LOCAL Genealogical Repositories** .... 26-27 • Check County Clerk & Courthouse for Local-level Death Records • Check for Local Newspaper-Obituary and other public records
Cemetery Association and Caretaker/Sexton Record	**Recommended Gen. Records/Resources Database Providers**.........27-29 • **Billion Graves** http://BillionGraves.com
Grave Opening Orders	→ App https://billiongraves.com/pages/help/mobiledevice.php
Interment Records	• **Find A Grave** www.FindAGrave.com

Tombstone/Headstone Records	→ App to find graves, add GPS, contribute + request headstone photos www.findagrave.com/mobileapp/ • **Interment.net** http://www.interment.net/Default.htmx • Check for Family Trees, Death Records, Military, etc. **Important U.S. Genealogical & Historical Societies**.................................29 • Check for Local Death Records and other record collections • Check for Bible and other Religious Records • Check for Members' Lineage and other Family Records

Description of Cemetery Records

Cemetery records are varied and valuable, often providing clues to vital records info, family groups, military service, religious and club memberships. Because of their value, many local genealogical/historical societies and other groups have gathered their info. Types of some U.S. cemeteries are: Religious Organization-owned, Government-owned, Private and Family/Farm.

Clues to other records in Cemetery Information might include:

🌿 Tombstones can often contain **fraternal organization symbols** signifying your ancestor's membership. Do a Google Image search to identify the symbols. Several of these fraternal organization are:

- **Ancient Order of Hibernians in America** ("AOH"), **Benevolent and Protective Order of Elks** ("BPOE"), **B-nai B'rith, Catholic Daughters of the Americas** ("CDA"), **Daughters of Isabella** ("DOI"), **Daughters of Rebekah, Fraternal Order of Eagles** ("FOE"), **Improved Order of Redmen** ("IORM"), **Independent Order of Odd Fellows** ("IOOF"), **Knights of Columbus** (K of C or KC), **Knights of Pythias** (K of P or KP), **Loyal Order of Moose** ("LOM"), **The Masonic Orders** [African-American Order of Shrine, The Blue Lodge ("AF&AM"), Daughters of Isis, The Order of the Eastern Star ("OES"), Prince Hall Masonry, Scottish Rite, Shrine ("SNA-AUM"), York Rite], **Modern Woodmen of America** ("MWA"), **Order of Sons of Italy in America** ("OSIA"), **Patrons of Husbandry** ("POH"), **PEO Sisterhood, Pocahontas, Pythian Sisters, Sons of Norway, Women of the Moose.**

Obtain Documents for Cemetery Records

🌿 Check the Cemetery Records chart above. Pay special attention to "**How To Find LOCAL Genealogical Repositories**" section (pages *26-27*).

🌿 **Locating Extant Cemeteries**: After identifying the geographic location, 1) Check Find A Grave https://www.findagrave.com/ and Billion Graves https://billiongraves.com/. If no luck, 2) Find location on FamilySearch Wiki https://familysearch.org/wiki/ or USGenWeb www.USGenWeb.com or in **Redbook** and look for cemetery info. If no luck, 3) Contact the local genealogical/historical society for that county. If no luck, 4) Check with your ancestor's religious denomination for cemetery records.

🌿 **Visiting a Cemetery:** Make sure to research online first, then do your homework before you go! 1) See their website or call about visiting hours, available records, etc. 2) Bring your ancestor's info. 3) Take pix.
- If you are at the cemetery and **can't read a tombstone**, take a digital photo using your smartphone, then "Edit" it with image filters along with manual controls of brightness, contrast or reverse negative.

🌿 *See the "**Cemetery Tools for genealogy**" section in **Fundamentals of Genealogy®: The Most Helpful Tools You've Never Used**.*

Recommended Guides To Cemetery Research In General

Recommended Guides To Cemetery Research In Their Collection

Recommended Textbooks for Cemetery Research

Basic U.S. Genealogical Records Group
Census Records . . .

Census Records	Census Records Locations + What To Check
U.S. Federal Censuses (1790-1930)	**Family Sources** .... *page 23* • Check for Location Clues in Family Papers and Relatives Interviews
U.S. Federal Non-Population / "Special Schedules"	**Important U.S. Nat'l & State Gen. Libraries, Repos. & Archives** .*24-26* • Check for Census Records and Tools
U.S. State, Town and Territorial Censuses	**How to Find LOCAL Genealogical Repositories** .... 26-27 • Check Local-level (usually State or Territorial) Census Records **Recommended Gen. Records/Resources Database Providers**....*27-29* • **Ancestry.com** – www.ancestry.com *(subscription service)* • **CyndisList** – "Census" www.cyndislist.com/census.htm • **FamilySearch** - https://familysearch.org/search • **HeritageQuest** *(possibly free thru your public library's online subscription)* www.ancestryheritagequest.com

Description of Census Records

Census records are quite possibly the most widely used genealogical research source since they contain information (considered "clues" until verified) for so many of our ancestors and are considered a "First Finding Source."

U.S. Federal Census Population Enumerations 1790-1940 are currently available to the public due to a 72-year privacy law (see the chart above).

🌿 Find NARA's U.S. Federal Census information plus extras in the left sidebar (listed below) at https://www.archives.gov/research/census
- About Census Records: 1940 Census, 1930 Census, 1850-1930 Census Clues, 1790-1840 Census Clues, Non-population Census, Indian Census Rolls, Presidents in the US Census Records, Census Links by Year
- Resources: Soundex Coding System, Blank Census forms and charts, Order Census Copies Online, Using Census Microfilm

🌿 To maximize your results, **consult a guide** (like *The Source* and FamilySearch Wiki) to determine which Censuses were taken in the locations of your ancestors' residence during their lifetime. Try to find them all.

🌿 **Getting Past Assumptions when searching & analyzing Census records:**
- Don't assume info was correct on the "Written Date" → It was correct on "Census Day" since the enumerator asked for info "on that date." See below.
- Don't assume all info was correct → Use Census info as clues until verified.
- Don't assume all children were descendants → Unless relationship stated.
- Don't assume all children's mother was the wife → Research to verify.
- Don't assume all people were related → Farmhands and others were listed.
- Don't assume the Head died → If the Head of Household changed, a younger member of the family often assumed that role since the former was elderly.
- Don't assume correct spellings → Use Soundex and multiple name spellings.

🌿 To fully understand the written responses, know the exact wording of each question. Find blank Census forms at NARA's "Resources for Genealogists >> Charts and Forms" https://www.archives.gov/research/genealogy/charts-forms.
- The 1940 U.S. Federal Census blank form has Explanatory Notes including how to correctly write the age of children under one year of age.

🌿 When an answer has been left blank, it means "Not Applicable" (not "Unsure").

🌿 Examine the entire Census page (margins, etc.) for possible valuable notes.

🌿 Quickly calculate people's ages in your head with two simple steps:
- Looking in 1900 Census for someone born in 1872; calculate in your head, "1900 minus 1872 equals 28."
- Get into the habit of saying, "**IF HE HAD A BIRTHDAY BEFORE CENSUS DAY** he was 28 years old; if not, he was 27."

Census Dates for "Day of Enumeration" or "Census Day" Listed By Year		
1790........ August 2, 1790	**1850** .... June 1, 1850	**1910**......... April 15, 1910
1800........ August 4, 1800	**1860** .... June 1, 1860	**1920**......... January 1, 1920
1810........ August 6, 1810	**1870** .... June 1, 1870	**1930**......... April 1, 1930
1820........ August 7, 1820	**1880** .... June 1, 1880	**1940**......... April 1, 1940
1830 .... June 1, 1830	**1890** .... June 2, 1890	
1840 .... June 1, 1840	**1900** .... June 1, 1900	

Soundex is a microfilmed card index that groups together surnames that are *pronounced* alike using a specialized letter-number code. Details are on the chart below. **Miracode** is a slightly modified version with index cards listing the household visitation numbers (used in the 1910 U.S. Federal Census).

	Soundex Code Deciphering Chart		
Step 1	The Soundex code consists of a letter (always the first letter of the surname) plus three numbers (assembles in Steps 2-9)		
Step 2	**Number**	**Represents Letters**	
	1	B P F V	
	2	C S G J K Q X Z	
	3	D T	
	4	L	
	5	M N	
	6	R	
Step 3	In coding your surname, disregard these letters: A, E, I, O, U, W, Y and H.		
Step 4	Double letters are treated as one letter.		
Step 5	On short names, if there are less than three numbers, add zeroes to the end of the coding so you have 1 letter and 3 numbers.		
Step 6	On long names, once you have three digits, disregard any additional ones.		
Step 7	If your surname has a prefix such as van, Van, Von, D', de, De, dela, Di, Du or Le, code it both with and without the prefix because it might be listed under either code.		
Step 8	Mc and Mac are not considered prefixes in the Soundex.		
Step 9	A Soundexed surname cannot have repeating numbers, so strike the second number and continue. For example, the surname "Jackson" Soundexes out at **J2225**, but since you have to eliminate the repeating number (the "2"s), Jackson becomes **J250**.		

❧ If you find an error in an online Census index, in the Help section find "Census index error" and see whether you can submit your corrections online.

❧ **Suggestions when you can't find your ancestor** in an online Census index:
  - Try another online Census index or finding aid. See the chart above.
  - If there was a State or other Census (including "Special Schedules"), find their residential address or neighbors, then find them in the U.S. Federal Census.
  - Check pagination of the Census . . . if there a page missing? If so, see if there's a different copy of that Census available (like State or Local) and also check for other Census (including Federal Agricultural, Industrial or Mortality).

🌿 Think past "the Census taker must have missed them" excuse and try some **Problem Solving Tips when searching online Census indexes:**
- <u>Common Surname</u> → Use birth info along with common surnames.
- <u>Common Surname</u> → Look for unusual first names to search.
- <u>Every Name Spelling</u> → Use Soundex, phonetics and wildcards.
- <u>Enumerator Mistakes</u> → Invert the first and last names.
- <u>Combine Unusual Family Details</u> → Find the family by searching for an individual's birth year + Mother's first name + Father's birthplace, etc.
- <u>Study handwriting</u> and try spelling substitutes.
- Use the alphabet <u>"Bump-Dangle-Point" deciphering method</u>.
- <u>Manually search</u> Census pages when you have neighborhood clues.
- <u>Find relatives</u>, then scan for your ancestor in that neighborhood.

🌿 **Other Censuses for U.S. Locations** – State, Town, Territorial, etc.

🌿 **"Special" U.S. Census Enumerations** - Population, Special Population (mortality, military schedule, etc.) and non-population (agriculture, industry, manufacturers, etc.). A few details:
- **Agriculture** – 1850-1880 lists owner/agent, livestock, produce, improvements, values, etc. (a farm was not included when in 1850-1860 it made less than $100 and in 1870-1880 it made less than $500).
- **Business Census of 1935** – The six schedules produced were advertising agencies, banking and financial institutions, public warehousing, radio broadcasting stations, motor trucking for fire, miscellaneous businesses.
- **Defective, Dependent & Delinquent Classes ("DDD")** – 1880 (if there's a check mark on the 1880 population schedule for DDD, go to this schedule): Insane inhabitants, Idiots, Deaf-mutes, Blind, Homeless Children, Inhabitants in Prison and Pauper and Indigent Inhabitants in Institutions, Poor-houses or Asylums or Boarded at Public Expense in Private Houses.
- **Industry** – 1850-1870 recorded owner, name of business, product, machines, employees by gender and age, wages, etc.
- **Manufactures** – 1820 recorded the names of the manufacturer, type of business, raw materials, goods produces, number of persons employed, etc. The 1880 Census expanded on the previous Industry Schedules by categorizing businesses, like "Boot and Shoe Factories" and "Coal Mines."
- **Mortality Schedules** – 1850-1880 taken separately from population censuses, listing those who died in the year preceding Census Day. They can list name, age, sex, race, marital status, birthplace, parents' foreign birth/length of U.S. residence, number of days ill, place where cause of death was contracted and name of attending physician, etc.
- **Slave Schedules** – 1850-1860 arranged by land owners, listed age, sex, color, sometimes names were listed, etc.

Clues to Census Information might be found in:

Birth/Marriage/Divorce/Death Records (Vital Records), Business Records, City & County Directories/Telephone Books, Military Records (including Draft Registration Cards), Newspapers-Obits, Naturalization, Social Security Applications & SSDI, etc.

Obtain Documents for Census Records

Recommended Guides To Census Research In General

Recommended Guides To Census Research In Their Collection

Recommended Textbooks for Census Research

Basic U.S. Genealogical Records Group
Death Records . . .

Death Records	Death Records Locations + What To Check
Burial Records	**Family Sources** .... *page 23*
Cemetery Records	• Check for Vital Records in Family Papers and Interviews with Relatives
Death Certificate-Civil & Religious	• Check for Bible and other Religious Records
	• Check for Bibliographis Sources
Death Record-Bible Entry	**Important U.S. Nat'l & State Gen. Libraries, Repos. & Archives** ...24-26
Death Record-Diary	• Check for State-level Vital Records
Death Record-Military	• Check for Bible & Religious Records or State Archives with their records
Death Register	**How to Find LOCAL Genealogical Repositories** 26-27
Funeral Records	• Check County Clerk & Courthouse for Local-level Vital Records
Newspaper-Death Notice & Obituary	• Check for Local Newspaper and other public records
	• Check for Local Religious Orgs or Archives with their records
Tombstone Records	**Recommended Gen. Records/Resources Database Providers**......27-29
Wills and Probate Records	• Check for Family Trees, Vital Records, Military, Naturalization, etc.
	Important U.S. Genealogical & Historical Societies............................29
	• Check for Local Vital Records and other record collections
	• Check for Bible and other Religious Records
	• Check for Members' Lineage and other Family Records

Description of Death Records

Death records are one of the four types of Vital Records. They have evolved with our country's growth, primarily in family and church records in early days,

Fundamentals of Genealogy®: Basics for Everyone

Second edition, part of the *Fundamentals of Genealogy*® textbook series

then later maintained by both the State and County governmental level. Their form and info differ greatly with the recording entity, location and time period.

- 🐚 You'll find State privacy laws surrounding Governmental Death Records. Check for records at both the State and County level. For early records, like most of New England, they might be found at the Town level.
- 🐚 The date availability of Governmental Death Records depends largely on when each State and County began requiring them.

Clues to Death Information might be found in:
Bibliographies, County Clerk's Records, Database Providers, Family Sources, Library Archives, Lineages on Social Media, Local Genealogical & Historical Societies, Newspapers-Death Notices & Obituaries, Religious Organizations, State Archives, State Department of Health Records, etc.

Obtain Documents for Death Records
- 🐚 **VitalRec.com** www.vitalrec.com/ leads you to the State and Local governmental vital records repositories. Choose "Death," then the State for date availability and fees. Proceed to the County (to check dates and fees). Varying State privacy laws apply.
- 🐚 Check the Death Records chart above. Pay special attention to the "**How To Find LOCAL Genealogical Repositories**" section (pages *26-27*).

Recommended Guides To Death Research In General

Recommended Guides To Death Research In Their Collection

Basic U.S. Genealogical Records Group
Directory Records – U.S. City, County and Phone . . .

Directory Records	Directory Records Locations + What To Check
U.S. City Directories	**Family Sources** .... *page 23*
U.S. County Directories	• Check for location info in Family Papers and Interviews with Relatives
U.S. Phone Directories- Business and Personal	**Important U.S. Nat'l & State Gen. Libraries, Repos. & Archives** ...*24-26* • Check for Directory Collections **How to Find LOCAL Genealogical Repositories** .... 26-27 • Check for Directory Collections **Recommended Gen. Records/Resources Database Providers**......*27-29* • Check for Directory Collections **Important U.S. Genealogical & Historical Societies**...........................*29* • Check for Directory Collections

Description of U.S. City, County and Phone Directory Records
Considered a "First Finding Source," paper Directories were the backbone of community information as the U.S. grew in the 19th and 20th Centuries. Early directories often gave much biographical plus family group information (including business details) and are well worth searching for. Even today, both paper and online directories give valuable identification clues.

🐾 Rule of thumb in Forensic Genealogy is that before our current "Information Age" where information is quickly obtained and published, old directories contained addresses that were recorded at least 6-9 months before the publication date of the directory.

🐾 Directories can contain:
  • Personal and Business information, including person's profession, business address (including intersection), residential address (including intersection), whether widow, other family members, etc.
  • A Street Directory
  • Schedules of Organizations

Obtain U.S. City, County And Phone Directory Records
🐾 Check the Directory Records chart above. Pay attention to the "**How To Find LOCAL Genealogical Repositories**" section (pages *26-27*).

Recommended Guides To Directory Research In General
🐾 Recommended Educational Resources.. 29-31
🐾 Recommended Genealogical Resources Organizations 29

Basic U.S. Genealogical Records Group
Divorce Records . . .

U.S. Divorce Records	Divorce Records Locations + What To Check
Divorce Records-Local County Court Records	**Family Sources** .... *page 23* • Check for Vital Records in Family Papers and Interviews with Relatives **How to Find LOCAL Genealogical Repositories** .... 26-27 • Check County Clerk & Courthouse for Local-level Vital Records **Recommended Gen. Records/Resources Database Providers** .....27-29 • Check for Family Trees, Vital Records, etc. **Important U.S. Genealogical & Historical Societies** ....29 • Check for Local Vital Records and other record collections

Descriptoin of Divorce Records

Divorce records are one of the four types of Vital Records. They are local court records whose form and info differ greatly with the recording entity, location and time period. There might be information about the divorcing couple, their children, professions, assets, their residences, possibly other relatives, etc. There seems to be a common misconception that divorce in the U.S. was rare until the late 20th Century; on the contrary, divorce was common in all American time periods and should be investigated in brick wall cases. Early divorce records can often contain a great deal of information and can provide clues to brick walls or unexplained "disappearances."

🍂 You'll find State privacy laws surrounding Governmental Birth Records. Check for records at both the State and County level. For early records, like most of New England, they might be found at the Town level.

🍂 The date availability of Governmental Birth Records depends largely on when each State and County began requiring them.

Clues To Divorce Info might be found *in Biographical information.*

Fundamentals of Genealogy®: Basics for Everyone

Second edition, part of the *Fundamentals of Genealogy®* textbook series

Obtain Documents for Divorce Records
- **VitalRec.com** www.vitalrec.com/ leads you to the State and Local governmental vital records repositories. Choose "Divorce Decree," then the State for date availability and fees. Proceed to the County (to check dates and fees). Varying State privacy laws apply.
- Check the Divorce Records chart above. Pay attention to the "**How To Find LOCAL Genealogical Repositories**" section (pages *26-27*).

Recommended Guides To Divorce Research In General

Recommended Guides To Divorce Research In Their Collection

Recommended Textbooks for Divorce Research

Basic U.S. Genealogical Records Group
Ethnic Records . . .

U.S. Ethnic Records	Ethnic Records Locations + What To Check
Ethnic Cemeteries Ethnic Club Records Ethnic Newspapers Ethnic Religious Records	**Family Sources** .... *page 23* • Check for Ethnicity Clues in Family Papers and Interviews with Relatives • Check for Religious and Cemetery Records • Check for Newspaper articles including those in Ethnic Newspapers • Check for Ethnic Club and Community Groups that may have records **How to Find LOCAL Genealogical Repositories** .... *26-27* • Check for Local Ethnic Groups that may have records • Check for Local Newspaper and other public records • Check for Local Library and Archives records for Ethnic groups **Recommended Gen. Records/Resources Database Providers** ......*27-29* • Check for Family Trees, Ethic Records, etc. **Important U.S. Genealogical & Historical Societies** ....*29* • Check for Local Ethic Records and other record collections • Check for Members' Lineage and other Family Records

Description of Ethnic Records
Search for the ethnic records since you might find biographical, cultural and social information for your ancestors and their family groups.

Obtain Documents for Ethnic Records
As defined by the Association of Professional Genealogists, these guidelines will give you a framework for conducting Ethnic Research:

- **"Identify Basic Resources"**
  - Find a genealogical society specializing in that ethnicity.
    - Google search for national and local societies.
    - CyndisList "Ethnic" www.cyndislist.com/cyndislistsearch/?q=ethnic.
    - Search Facebook for these national and local societies.
  - Find a FamilySearch Wiki www.FamilySearch.org/wiki article or guide.
- **"Study the History, Religion and Culture"**
  - Review historical events to see if they affected your ancestors. Check history books, atlases of history, etc.
  - Identify the primary or state religion for possible records.
- **"Learn the Geography"**
  - Collect and study maps, gazetteers, land records, etc. . . *see "**Maps and Gazetteers**" section in "**Some Basic Genealogical Tools**."*
  - Google for information on Countries' boundary changes.
- **"Use Language Tools"**
  - Simple word translations (such as deciphering printed words on a form) from Google Translate https://translate.google.com/
  - Ask for help on Facebook group pages.
- Check the Ethnic Records chart above. Pay special attention to the "**How To Find LOCAL Genealogical Repositories**" section (pages *26-27*).

Recommended Guides To Ethnic Research In General

Recommended Guides To Ethnic Research In Their Collection

Recommended Textbooks for Ethnic Research

Basic U.S. Genealogical Records Group
Funeral Records . . .

U.S. Funeral Records	Funeral Records Locations + What To Check
Family Source-Funeral Cards, Programs & Attendance Books	**Family Sources** .... *page 23* • Check for Death Records in Family Papers and Interviews with Relatives • Check for Bible and other Religious Records
Funeral Home Records	**How to Find LOCAL Genealogical Repositories** .... *26-27* • Check whether the Funeral Home still exists or where their records are • Check for Local Newspaper and other public records **Recommended Gen. Records/Resources Database Providers**......*27-29* • Check for Family Trees, Death Records, etc. **Important U.S. Genealogical & Historical Societies**............................*29* • Check for Local Death Records and other record collections • Check for Local Funeral Home Records • Check for Members' Lineage and other Family Records

Description of Funeral Records
Funeral Records are a type of Death Record (which is one of the four types of Vital Records). They may contain Age at death, Date of interment or cremation, Place of interment, Location of burial plot, Local newspaper death notice and/or obituary, Payee (possible relationship), Pallbearers (possible relationship), Surviving and sometimes deceased family members.

Clues to Funeral Information might be found *in Home Sources, Cemetery Records, Death Records (like Death Certificates), Death Notices & Obits.*

Obtain Documents for Funeral Records
❧ Google the Funeral Home to see if it still exists and has any records.
❧ If the Funeral Home no longer exists, search Local sources for the archival records.
❧ If you don't know the name of the Funeral Home, find Clues (above). If still no luck, find historic directory sources for the location for clues.
❧ Check the Funeral Records chart above. Pay special attention to the **"How to Find LOCAL Genealogical Repositories"** section (pages *26-27*).

Recommended Guides To Funeral Research In General
❧ Recommended Educational Resources.. 29-31
❧ Recommended Genealogical Resources Organizations 29

Recommended Guides To Funeral Research In Their Collection

Basic U.S. Genealogical Records Group
Immigration Records . . .

U.S. Immigration Records	Immigration Records Locations + What To Check
Ship's Passenger Lists or Manifests	**Family Sources** .... *page 23* • Check for Immigration details in Family Papers and Interviews • Check for Naturalization documents that might give Immigration details **Important U.S. Nat'l & State Gen. Libraries, Repos. & Archives** ...*24-26* • Check for National Immigration Records **Recommended Gen. Records/Resources Database Providers**......*27-29* • Check Immigratoin Records, Naturalization, etc. **Important U.S. Genealogical & Historical Societies**............................*29* • Check for Immigratoin and other record collections

Find the **Naturalization Petition** before searching Immigration Records . . .
it will often provide you with all of the immigration details!

Description of Immigration Records

Passenger lists weren't required when arriving in a U.S. port until 1820 when a pre-printed form had to be completed for each passenger documenting their name, age and sex. More information was required in later decades which may include Immigrant's Name and Birthplace, Former Residence(s), Dates of Embarkation and Arrival, Ports, Who they were traveling with, etc.
- *Part One = "Oath of Allegiance"*
- *Part Two = "Declaration of Intention"*
- *Part Three = "Petition for Naturalization"*

Clues to Immigration Information *might be found in Home Sources (including family lore, bibles, photo albums, old letters with locations/ postmarks), Vital Records (especially important are birth/marriage/death certificates, biography, obituary, diary records) and Census Records after 1900 have a column listing "Year of Immigration to the United States."*

Obtain Documents for Immigration Records

1. Check www.EllisIsland.org (if passengers arrived at New York port between 1982-1943) and print directly from the online manifest images;
2. OR, once you've searched indexes (either in paper volumes or online at Olive Tree Genealogy and the links at CyndisList) and found the identity of possible ships' passenger and customs' passenger lists/manifest names:
   a. Order and view microfilm from:
      i. NARA and view it at the local NARA-Regional Archives, or
      ii. LDS and view it at a local Family History Center or the Newberry Library;
   b. OR, order NARA takes orders for searches/photocopies by mail using NATF Form 81 www.archives.gov/research/order (you must at least know passenger's full name, U.S. port of arrival and month/year of arrival).
3. OR, subscribe to Ancestry.com's "U.S. Immigration Collection, NY Passenger Lists, 1851-1891" and print directly from the online manifest images.

🔖 **If that fails, check Ships' Customs/Passenger Lists/Manifests INDEXES:** Once you have an idea of the date and location of your immigrant ancestor's port arrival in the U.S., check William P. Filby's, *Passenger and Immigration Lists Index* (a series that is a finding aid to published passenger lists - available at the Newberry Library and on CD-ROM from Broderbund).

   U.S. Ports: Major indexes exist for — Baltimore, 1820-1952 • Boston, 1848-1891 and 1902-1920 • New Orleans, 1853-1952 • New York City, 1820-1846 and 1892-1943 (Castle Garden=1855-1891; Ellis Island 1892-1943) • Philadelphia 1800-1948 • Minor ports, 1820-1874 & 1890-1924

🔖 **National Archives & Records Administration Microfilm:** See their webpage at www.archives.gov/genealogy/immigration. A general overview and more information is at www.archives.gov/genealogy/immigration/passenger-arrival.html. Contrary to popular belief, NARA does not have copies of all ship passenger lists. Check their *Immigrant and Passenger Arrivals: A Select Catalog of National Archives Microfilm Publications* www.archives.gov/publications/genealogy/microfilm-catalogs.html. It **does** have the following microfilm — Beginning in 1800 for Philadelphia • Beginning in 1820 for most East Coast and Gulf Coast ports • A great many (but not all) ships' passenger lists from 1891-1954 for the ports above. Phone your Regional NARA to see if they already have this microfilm on site; if not, they can order it for you to view within 4-6 weeks.

🍃 **If you can't find your ancestor in any immigrant and passenger indexes . . .** consider the following: • Check all the U.S. Federal Census enumerations for your ancestor . . . • Consider whether the name you should be looking for was in a foreign language . . . • Consider whether women's names were listed as married or maiden . . . • Check ports other than New York . . . • Check transcribed directories like Filby's and the "Morton Allan Directory" . . . • See whether you can obtain any more family stories information . . . • Check City Directories to track your ancestor back in time to pinpoint the year of arrival in that city . . . • Check other types of record for clues, like Obituaries, Death Certificates, Military Records, etc.

🍃 Check the Immigration Records chart above. Pay attention to the "**How To Find LOCAL Genealogical Repositories**" section (pages *26-27*).

Some Websites for Immigration Records

🍃 Ancestry.com's www.ancestry.com (subscription service) "U.S. Immigration Collection, NY Passenger Lists, 1851-1891"

🍃 CyndisList – "Immigration & Naturalization"

🍃 CyndisList - "Ships & Passenger Lists" www.cyndislist.com/ships.htm

🍃 CyndisList – "Ports of Entry" www.cyndislist.com/portsentry.htm

🍃 CyndisList – "Ellis Island" www.cyndislist.com/ellis.htm

🍃 Ellis Island Database www.ellisisland.org

🍃 LDS Online Catalog Search www.familysearch.org

🍃 NARA Immigration www.archives.gov/genealogy/immigration

🍃 NARA's *Microfilm Publications* www.archives.gov/publications/genealogy/microfilm-catalogs.html

🍃 NARA's Order Online www.archives.gov/research/order/orderonline.html

🍃 NARA's Passenger List Photocopy Order Form www.archives.gov/contact/inquire-form.html

🍃 Olive Tree Genealogy - Free tutorials and guides to immigration and ships' passenger list www.olivetreegenealogy.com

🍃 Steve Morse's Immigration – www.stevemorse.org and One-Step Ellis Island search forms www.jewishgen.org/databases/EIDB/intro.html

Recommended Guides To Immigration Research In General

Recommended Guides To Immigration Research In Their Collection

Basic U.S. Genealogical Records Group

<u>Land Records</u> . . .

U.S. Land Records	Land Records Locations + What To Check
Deed of Gift (Land)	**Family Sources** .... *page 23*
Deed of Sale (Land)	• Check for Locations in Vital Records in Family Papers and Interviews
Estate Settlement	• Check for Locations in Biographical Sources, Census, Obits, Tax, etc.
Land Abstract	**Important U.S. Nat'l & State Gen. Libraries, Repos. & Archives** ...*24-26*
Land Entry Case File	• Check for BLM Land Records (if your ancestor was a Patentee)
Land Patent Case File	• Check for State-level Land Records
Mortgage Sale	**How to Find LOCAL Genealogical Repositories** *26-27*
	• Check County Clerk & County Land Assessor for Local Land Records
	• Check for Local Newspaper and other public records
	Recommended Gen. Records/Resources Database Providers......*27-29*
	• Check for Family Trees, Vital Records, Land, Census, etc.
	Important U.S. Genealogical & Historical Societies.......... *29*
	• Check for Local Landl Records and other record collections

Description of Land Records

Land records, issued by the U.S. federal and county courts, can provide reliable info on the family members, social status, occupation, neighbors, etc. Early land deeds are especially detailed and predate most other record sources. Land records can be especially important since they often involve a group of people (who were possibly related), confirm a person resided at a certain location at a certain time, they can help distinguish between like-named ancestors, etc. They may contain: Names of all parties in the transaction, Location of residence(s), Relationships of parties.

- **Land Patent** = the first transfer of a piece of property from some government entity into the hands of an individual.
- **Land Grant** = the transfer of property from one individual to another, and covers pretty much all land transactions following the original <u>patent</u>.
- **Land Deed** = a legal instrument conveying transfer which includes a warranty deed by which the seller warrants (guarantees) the title to the <u>land being sold</u>.
- **State-Land States** = 20 states in all . . . Connecticut, Delaware, Georgia,

Hawaii, Kentucky, Maine, Maryland, Massachusetts, New Hampshire, New Jersey, New York, North Carolina, Pennsylvania, Rhode Island, South Carolina, Tennessee, Texas, Vermont, Virginia, West Virginia . . . they have various surveying systems . . .

- **Public-Domain States** = the other 30 states. . . Alabama, Alaska, Arizona, Arkansas, California, Colorado, Florida, Idaho, Illinois, Indiana, Iowa, Kansas, Louisiana, Michigan, Minnesota, Mississippi, Missouri, Montana, Nebraska, Nevada, New Mexico, North Dakota, Ohio, Oklahoma, Oregon, South Dakota, Utah, Washington, Wisconsin, and Wyoming. The original thirteen colonies, plus Kentucky, Maine, Tennessee, Texas, Vermont, and later West Virginia and Hawaii . . . use the federal township and range system and include a special subcategory called private land claims . . .
  - **Rectangular Survey System of Public Lands:** One of the biggest differences between land in the public land states and state land states is that public land was surveyed prior to being made available for purchase or homesteading, using the *rectangular-survey system*, otherwise known as the township-range system. When a survey was done on new public land, two lines were run at right angles to each other through the territory - a *base line* running east and west and a *meridian line* running north and south. The land was then divided into sections from the point of this intersection as follows:
  - **Township & Range** - Townships, a major subdivision of public lands under the rectangular survey system, measure approx. 6 miles on a side (36 square miles). Townships are then numbered from the base line north and south and then from the meridian line east and west. The east/west identification is known as the Range. A Township is identified by this relationship to a base line and a principal meridian. Example: *Township 3 North, Range 9 West, 5th Principal Meridian* identifies a specific township that is 3 tiers north from the base line and 9 tiers west (Range) of the 5th Principal Meridian.
  - **Section Number** - Townships were then further broken down into thirty-six sections of 640 acres each (one square mile) called sections, which were numbered with reference to the base line and meridian line.
- **Land Entry Case Files:** Before the individuals received patents, some gov. paperwork was necessary. Those purchasing land from the U.S. had to be given receipts for payments, while those obtaining land through military bounty land warrants, preemption entries, or the Homestead Act of 1862, had to file applications, give proof about military service, residence on and improvements to the land, or proof of citizenship. The paperwork generated by those bureaucratic activities, compiled into land entry case files, is held by NARA.
- **U.S. County Boundaries:** You must determine whether there were any County Boundary changes between the time your ancestor lived in a location and today so you search in the right place (see "**Some Basic Genealogical Tools**").

Clues to Land Information *might be found in Family Sources, Biographical Sources, Census, Obituary, Tax Records, etc.*

Obtain Documents for Land Records

1. Local Land Assessor, Courthouses or County Clerk's Offices.

2. Bureau of Land Management – At www.blm.gov for online public-domain land patents (original transfer from government to individual).

🐾 Check the Land Records chart above. Pay special attention to the "**How To Find LOCAL Genealogical Repositories**" section (pages *26-27*).

Recommended Guides To Land Research In General

Recommended Guides To Land Research In Their Collection

Basic U.S. Genealogical Records Group
Marriage Records . . .

U.S. Marriage Records	Marriage Records Locations + What To Check
Marriage Bann	**Family Sources** .... *page 23*
Marriage Bond	• Check for Vital Records in Family Papers and Interviews with Relatives
Marriage Certificate-Civil & Government	• Check for Bible and other Religious Records **Important U.S. Nat'l & State Gen. Libraries, Repos. & Archives** ...*24-26*
Marriage Consent	• Check for State-level Vital Records
Marriage License	• Check for Bible and other Religious Records
Marriage Record-Bible	**How to Find LOCAL Genealogical Repositories** 26-27
Marriage Record-Military	• Check County Clerk & Courthouse for Local-level Vital Records
Marriage Registration	• Check for Local Newspaper and other public records **Recommended Gen. Records/Resources Database Providers**......*27-29*
	• Check for Family Trees, Vital Records, Military, Naturalization, etc.
	Important U.S. Genealogical & Historical Societies...........................*29*
	• Check for Local Vital Records and other record collections
	• Check for Bible and other Religious Records
	• Check for Members' Lineage and other Family Records

Description of Marriage Records

Marriage records are one of the four types of Vital Records. They have evolved with our country's growth, primarily in family and church records in early days, then later maintained by both the State and County governmental level. Their form and info differ greatly with the recording entity, location and time period. Marriage licenses are the most common marriage records for all U.S. time periods. Marriage certificates were often given to the couple after the ceremony and are usually found among family records. Always check for the marriage license application, not just for certificates and filed returns.

- You'll find State privacy laws surrounding Governmental Marriage Records. Check for records at both the State and County level. For early records, like most of New England, they might be found at the Town level.
- The date availability of Governmental Marriage Records depends largely on when each State and County began requiring them.
- **Marriage Banns** . . . usually read in church on three consecutive Sundays, or posted in public places, or published in newspapers . . . this was a common church custom in Early (Protestant) America.
- **Marriage Bonds** . . . an amount of money posted to the court by a representative of the groom (customarily the bride's father or brother) to defray the cost of litigation in the event the marriage was nullified.
- **Consent Affidavits** . . . a parent or legal guardian of an underage bride or groom attested their written permission for the wedding . . . in some instances this permission was written directly on a marriage certificate.
- Many genealogists eagerly seek these vital records since they often provide the maiden name of female ancestors, and possible also: Affidavits of witnesses can show relationships, Under-age consent affidavits can show a direct parent-child relationship (which goes far in parental relationship proofs!) and if a military ceremony it may provide the serviceman's complete service identification.

Clues to Marriage Information might be found *in Family Sources, Census, Club Records, Death Records (Cemetery, Tombstone, Funeral), Directories, Newspaper and Obit, Land Records, Will/Probate Records, etc.*

Obtain Documents for Marriage Records
1. Since U.S. Marriage Certificates are usually at State and County Clerk's offices, use **VitalRec.com** www.vitalrec.com/. Choose "Marriage," then the State for date availability and fees. Proceed to the County (to check dates and fees). Varying State privacy laws apply.
2. Religious marriage records can be found at the local church or archives.
- Marriage Records take many forms. So check the chart above, "**How To Find LOCAL Genealogical Repositories**" section (pages 26-27).

Basic U.S. Genealogical Records Group
Military Records . . .

U.S. Military Records	Military Records Locations + What To Check
Adjutant General's Reports	**Family Sources** .... *page 23*
Compiled Service Record	• Check for Military Info in Family Papers and Interviews with Relatives
Discharge Papers	**Important U.S. Nat'l & State Gen. Libraries, Repos. & Archives** ...*24-26*
Draft Registration Cards	• Check for NARA Military Records *(see below)*
Manuscript Materials	• State-level Military Records
Military Burial Cards	**How to Find LOCAL Genealogical Repositories** 26-27
Muster Rolls	• Check for Local Newspaper and other public records
Pension File	**Recommended Gen. Records/Resources Database Providers**......*27-29*
Personnel Indexes	• Check for Military Records (also see below)
Regimental Histories	**Important U.S. Genealogical & Historical Societies**...........................29
Widow's Pension File	• Check for Local Military Records and other record collections
	• Check for Bible and other Religious Records
	• Check for Members' Military Ancestors and other Family Records

Description of Military Records
Military records can be biographical and revealing! They differ greatly with time and location. Miscellaneous Military Records include pay rolls, hospital records, prison-of-war records, promotions, court martial, draft records, etc.

🌿 **Clues to Military Information** might be found in Guide suggestions like search online newspapers during that time period for various lists of draft exemptees, soldiers by unit, those Killed In Action, pensioners, etc.

Outline of U.S. Military Conflicts that might produce records for Service Personnel & Aid Workers

1675-1676	King Philip's War (militiamen primarily from Connecticut, Massachusetts and Rhode Island)
1676	Bacon's Rebellion (Virginia)
1689-1697	King William's War/War of the League of Augsburg
1702-1713	Queen Anne's War/War of the Spanish Succession
1715-1716	Yamasee War (South Carolina and Georgia)
1739-1742	War of Jenkins' Ear (Georgia and Florida)
1744-1748	King George's War/War of Austrian Succession
1754-1763	French and Indian War/Seven Years War
1760-1761	Cherokee Uprising (North and South Carolina)
1763-1764	Pontiac's Rebellion (militiamen primarily from Pennsylvania, Maryland and Virginia)
1771	War of the Regulators (North Carolina)
1774	Lord Dunmore's War (Virginia, Pennsylvania and Ohio)
1775-1783	American Revolutionary War
1786-1787	Shays Rebellion (Massachusetts)
1794	Whiskey Rebellion (Pennsylvania)
1798-1800	Quasi-war with France (Atlantic Coast and West Indies)
1801-1805	War with the Barbary Pirates
1811	Battle of Tippecanoe (Indiana)
1812-1815	War of 1812
1817-1819	Seminole War
1831-1832	Black Hawk War (Midwest)
1835-1842	Second Seminole War/Florida War
1836	Texas War of Independence
1839	Aroostook War (Maine)
1841	Door Rebellion (Rhode Island)
1846-1848	Mexican War
1846-1868	Navajo Wars (New Mexico and Arizona)
1848-1858	Third Seminole War
1855-1858	Yakima Wars (Washington, Oregon and Idaho)
1857-1858	Utah War
1861-1865	U.S. Civil War
1866-1890	Sioux and Cheyenne Wars (Dakotas and Montana)
1870-1886	Apache Wars (Arizona, New Mexico and Mexico)
1872-1873	Modoc War (California)
1877	Nez Perce Ward (Idaho and Montana)
1898	Spanish-American War
1899-1902	Philippine Insurrection
1900	Boxer Rebellion (China)
1914	Tampico and Vera Cruz Incidents (Mexico)
1916-1917	Mexican Punitive Expedition (search for Pancho Villa)
1917-1918	World War I
1941-1945	World War II
1950-1953	Korean Conflict
1961-1973	Vietnam War
1990-1991	Persian Gulf War
2003-	Iraq War

Obtain Documents for Military Records

Try local/state, then national sources. There are many online digitized records and indexes to help you track down the original record quickly.

- **Allen County Public Library Genealogy Center's "Our Military Heritage" Database** www.genealogycenter.info/military/
- **Ancestry®'s Military Records Collections** *(subscription service)*

- 🌿 **Access to Archival Databases ("AAD")** http://aad.archives.gov/aad
- 🌿 **Daughters of the American Revolution's Genealogical Research System** http://services.dar.org/public/dar_research/search/?tab_id=0
- 🌿 **Fold3's Military Records** https://www.Fold3.com
- 🌿 **U.S. Library Of Congress ("LOC")** https://www.LOC.gov
- 🌿 **U.S. National Archives and Records Admin. ("NARA")** "Research in Military Records" https://www.archives.gov/veterans (or obtain copies of the following records via mail National Archives and Records, Administration, Att: NWDT1, 700 Pennsylvania Avenue, NW, Washington, DC 20408-0001). Order forms https://www.archives.gov/forms as below:
  - NATF Form 85 – **Military Pension/Bounty Land Warrant Appl.**
  - NATF Form 86 – **(Pre-WWI) Military Service Records**
  - Form SF 180 – **(Post-WWI) Military Records.**
    - To obtain military personnel records for 20th Century servicemen (this included medical information) that were not destroyed in the fire. **National Personnel Records Center** at https://www.archives.gov/st-louis (or write NPRC, Military Personnel Records, 1 Archives Drive, St. Louis, MO 63138).
  - For all others, your request is best made using a **Standard Form 180.**
- 🌿 Check the Military Records chart above. Pay special attention to the "**How To Find LOCAL Genealogical Repositories**" section (pages *26-27).*

Recommended Guides To Military Research In General

Recommended Guides To Military Research In Their Collection

Recommended Textbooks for Military Research

Basic U.S. Genealogical Records Group
Naturalization Records . . .

U.S. Naturalization Records	Naturalization Records Locations + What To Check
"Oath of Allegiance"	**Family Sources** .... *page 23*

"Declaration of Intention"	• Check for Records in Family Papers and Interviews with Relatives
"Petition for Naturalization"	• Check for Biographical Records
	Important U.S. Nat'l & State Gen. Libraries, Repos. & Archives ...*24-26*
	• Check for NARA Naturalization Records *(see below)*
	How to Find LOCAL Genealogical Repositories 26-27
	• Check County Courthouse Naturalization Lists and Records
	Recommended Gen. Records/Resources Database Providers......*27-29*
	• Check Ancestry.com's Naturalization Records Indexes *(see below)*.
	Important U.S. Genealogical & Historical Societies 29
	• Check for Naturalization Records Collections
	• Check for Members' Lineage and other Family Records

Find the **Naturalization Petition** before searching Immigration Records . . .
it will often provide you with all of the immigration details!

Description of Naturalization Records

*Most U.S. Naturalizations included two steps: **1)** The original filing of an application in court is called a **"Declaration of Intent"** (also called the "first papers"). There was a three-year waiting period before Step Two. Some of the best information you will find is on these first papers. **2)** A second filing of an application in court (after the three-year waiting period) is called a **"Petition for Naturalization."** During some time periods, aliens were asked to sign a precursory **"Oath of Allegiance."** In Colonial Days, this court document might be all you can find (and may simply have name & signature).*

🕊 **From 1790-1922 WIVES** were granted "derivative citizenship" through their husband's naturalization. In most cases before September 1906, there was little, if any, information about the wife in the husband's naturalization documents. (Therefore, after 1922 each individual had to file their own naturalization paperwork.)

🕊 **From 1790-1940** children (under the age of 21) were granted "derivative citizenship" through their father's naturalization. In most cases before 1906, there was little, if any, information about children in the father's naturalization documents.
- However, **from 1824-1906** children were allowed to file their own "Declaration" and "Petition" **at the same time** if they had lived in the U.S. for five years before their 23rd birthday.

🕊 **After September 27, 1906.** While naturalization proceedings could have taken place in any U. S. District Court, or in any court of record, all proceedings were required to be recorded by the clerk of the court and a copy sent to a central office maintained by Immigration and Naturalization Service ("INS"), 425 I Street, NW., Washington, DC 20520.

🕊 During all time periods (with the possible exception of wartime), an alien woman who married a male U.S. citizen automatically became a U.S. citizen (so as not needing to file naturalization paperwork). Conversely, an American woman who married an alien lost her U.S. citizenship rights. These practices stopped in the 1950's with law change.

Clues to Naturalization Information *might be found in Census Records and Home Sources (including family lore, bibles, photo albums, old letters with locations/ postmarks), Vital Records (especially important are birth/marriage/death certificates, biography, obituary, diary records).*

Obtain Documents for Naturalization Records

1. Check **local courts**, regional federal courts and local/state archives. Start in your ancestor's county in USGenWeb http://usgenweb.org/ or FamilySearch Wiki https://familysearch.org/wiki/.
2. Check **Ancestry.com's U.S. Naturalization Records Indexes** https://www.ancestry.com/ *(subscription service)*
3. With your ancestor's index entry, find the Naturalization court location in the FamilySearch Catalog https://familysearch.org/catalog/search or call your NARA Regional Facility https://www.archives.gov/locations
4. For further resources, **NARA's "Naturalization Introduction"** www.archives.gov/genealogy/naturalization "Where to Find Naturalization Records" www.archives.gov/genealogy/naturalization/#find
🐚 Check the Naturalization Records chart above. Pay attention to the "**How to Find LOCAL Genealogical Repositories**" section (pages *26-27*).

Recommended Guides To Naturalization Research In General

Recommended Guides To Naturalization Research In Their Collection

Recommended Textbooks for Naturalization Research

Basic U.S. Genealogical Records Group
Newspaper Records . . .

U.S. Newspaper Records	Newspaper Records Locations + What To Check
Advertisements	**Family Sources** .... *page 23*
Anniversary Articles	• Check for Newspaper Clippings in Family Papers and Interview Clues
Announcements-Birth	**Important U.S. Nat'l & State Gen. Libraries, Repos. & Archives** ...24-26
Announcements-Business	• Check for State-level Newspaper Collections (including on microfilm)
Death Notices	**How to Find LOCAL Genealogical Repositories** 26-27
Engagement Announcemts	• Check Local Libraries *(also see below)*
Family Reunion Articles	**Recommended Gen. Records/Resources Database Providers**......27-29
Fraternal & Club Events	• Check Ancestry, FamilySearch and USGenWeb *(also see below)*
Military Articles	• Check Newspapers.com, etc. *(also see below)*
News Items and Miscellany	**Important U.S. Genealogical & Historical Societies**............................29
Obituaries	• Check for Local Newspaper Collections
Wedding Announcement	

Description of Newspaper Records

Newspapers can provide insightful details on ancestors who lived in the 18th-20th centuries, especially in rural communities. Along with the common birth, marriage and death notices, business and personal advertisements, researchers often find the illness of family members, voter and jury lists, school and social events, church and fraternal organizations' functions, political meetings, along with news pertaining to merchants and the movers and shakers of the community. Many newspapers have been microfilmed and can be obtained on interlibrary loan. Even easier are the many newspapers that have been digitized and are accessible online. Some tips follow:

Clues found in Newspaper Information might include:

🐛 Obituaries might list your ancestor's fraternal organizations, often only abbreviated. *See the "Cemetery Records" section for a list of possible fraternal organizations.*

Obtain Newspaper Records

The easiest Newspaper sources to find are online digitized and microfilmed. Networking and Genealogical & Historical Society collections might provide clippings or abstracts/extracts. Try to find both types of Newspaper Records!
1. Try online Newspapers databases and archives.
- America's Obituaries & Death Notices *(possibly thru your public library)*
- Ancestry®'s Newspapers Collection *(subscription service)*

- CyndisList "Newspapers" www.cyndislist.com/newspapers
- CyndisList "Obituaries" www.cyndislist.com/obituaries
- GenealogyBank www.genealogybank.com/ *(subscription service)*
- Newspapers.com https://www.newspapers.com/ *(subscription service)*

2. Allen County Public Library "Newspapers on Microfilm" www.genealogy center.org/Pathfinders/NewspaperMicrofilm.aspx#Section10
   - **Facebook "Free Obituary Look-Ups"** private group https://www.facebook.com/groups/FREEOBITUARYLOOKUPS/
   - Find today's world newspapers **Mondo Times** www.mondotimes.com/. Search each newspaper's website for Obituaries they make available (often in their Archives, many have not yet been digitized).
   - To find the **newspapers published in your ancestor's location during their lifetime**, check USGenWeb http://usgenweb.org/ or FamilySearch Wiki https://familysearch.org/wiki/.
   - **To find microfilm**, search check USGenWeb http://usgenweb.org/ FamilySearch Wiki https://familysearch.org/wiki/ and CyndisList http://www.cyndislist.com/micro/ at the county and state levels.
   - Once you've located microfilm, check whether your public library can do an Inter-Library Loan. If ordering it from FamilySearch.org, use a Family History Center https://familysearch.org/locations/
- ❧ Check the Newspaper Records chart above. Pay attention to the "**How To Find LOCAL Genealogical Repositories**" section (pages *26-27*).

Recommended Guides To Newspaper Research In General

Recommended Guides To Newspaper Research In Their Collection

Recommended Textbooks for Newspaper Research

Basic U.S. Genealogical Records Group
Religious Records . . .

U.S. Religious Records	Religious Records Locations + What To Check
Address/Biographical Info	**Family Sources** ....*page 23*

Baptism Records	• Check for Religious Records in Family Papers and Interviews with Relatives
Bible Records	• Check for Bible and other Religious Records
Burial Records	**Important U.S. Nat'l & State Gen. Libraries, Repos. & Archives** 24-26
Cemetery Records	• Check for Religious Denomination Records at Archives
Death Records	**How to Find LOCAL Genealogical Repositories** 26-27
Directory of Members	• Check City & County Local-level Religious Records at Extant Organizations
Funeral Records	• Check for Local Newspaper and other public records for clues to prior religious bodies
Marriage Records	**Recommended Gen. Records/Resources Database Providers** 27-29
Membership Lists	• Check for Religious Records, Vital Records, Cemetery, Funeral, etc.
Minutes of Membership Meetings	**Important U.S. Genealogical & Historical Societies** 29
	• Check for Local Religious Records and other record collections
	• Check for Members' Lineage and other Family Records

Description of Religious Records
Many of our ancestors left numerous religious records since these records were created for their life events. And don't overlook it as a profession.

Clues to Religious Information might be found:
One way to determine the religious affiliations of your ancestors is to search through Obituaries, Cemetery Records and Biographical Sources. Pay attention to family traditions, children's names, marriage returns, the style, translation and language of old family Bibles or other religious books.

🐌 Search the **(U.S.) 1926 Census of Religious Bodies** (currently downloadable at http://www.ebooks-downloads.net/ebook-pdf/census-of-religious-bodies-1926) for your ancestor's location. This volume lists religious organizations, not individuals, for "Every identifiable denomination, based on lists of churches and religious organizations from yearbooks, denominations, and other sources . . ."

Obtain Documents for Religious Records
1. Try to **Identify the Religious Affiliation** and search for local religious institutions in your ancestor's location at that time (check histories of local organizations in that location today and also "Directory Records").
2. Search for **local Religious Cemeteries** – try to obtain their Cemetery Records or Tombstone Inscriptions.
3. Search for **Religious Denomination Headquarters** for archives info.
4. Search **Religious Records database collections**:
   • **Allen County Public Library Genealogy Center's "Family Bible Records" Database** www.genealogycenter.info/bibles/
   • **Ancestry®'s** Record Collections (search by record type and location)
   • CyndisList "**Religion**" www.cyndislist.com/cyndislistsearch/?q=religion

- FamilySearch.org's Records and Books https://familysearch.org/search
🌿 Check the Religious Records chart above. Pay attention to the "**How To Find LOCAL Genealogical Repositories**" section (pages *26-27*).

Basic U.S. Genealogical Records Group
Tax Records . . .

U.S. Tax Records	Tax Records Locations + What To Check
Federal or Personal Income Tax Records	**Family Sources** .... *page 23* • Check for Clues in Family Papers and Interviews with Relatives
Head Tax Records	**How to Find LOCAL Genealogical Repositories** 26-27
Personal Property Tax	• Check County Clerk for Local-level Tax Records
Poll Tax	• Check Courthouse or Land Assessor for Property Tax Records
Personal Property Tax *(might include Head of Household, Dependents, Income Property-Ownership or Rental, Livestock, Farming Implements, Household Goods, etc.)*	**Recommended Gen. Records/Resources Database Providers**......27-29 • Check for Tax Records, etc. **Important U.S. Genealogical & Historical Societies**............................29 • Check for Local Tac Records and other record collections • Check for Bible and other Religious Records • Check for Members' Lineage and other Family Records

Description of Tax Records
Tax records can give researchers a wealth of information in two ways, telling us of taxable property/business record and also establish our ancestors' residency when other records have been destroyed. To have a thorough understanding of who might and might not appear on tax lists (like the taxable age, gender & ethnicity laws, etc.), consult a local history for the time.

※ In the early U.S., **Poll Tax or Head Tax** (a tax per person), compiled by a local government, was common and many lists are extant today. Although they typically don't list much detail, they can help:
- Establish residency for an ancestor at a certain time and location;
- Establish the number of persons in the household at a given time;
- Determine when sons "became of age" (usually at 16 – when they were considered "taxable males");
- Determine when a wife was newly widowed since she took over as the Head of the Household on the Tax Rolls.

※ **Personal Property and Real Estate Tax Rolls**, also compiled by a local government, can list significant detail and were often created annually (so they can reflect family change when compared over a period of time).

※ **Personal Federal Income Tax**, was first taken by the U.S. Internal Revenue Service in 1914. However, digitized Income Tax Records (1862-1872) images are available at FamilySearch.org.

Obtain Documents for Tax Records
1. Check **Local Genealogical & Historical Society** tax records collection.
2. **Local Government** (especially county courthouses, state archives, etc.)
3. Check **online databases** and records collections:
   - CyndisList "**Taxes**" www.cyndislist.com/taxes
   - **FamilySearch.org** www.familysearch.org/ tax records [including digitized Income Tax Records (1862-1872) images].

※ Check the Tax Records chart above. Pay special attention to the "**How To Find LOCAL Genealogical Repositories**" section (pages *26-27*).

Recommended Guides To Tax Research In General

Recommended Guides To Tax Research In Their Collection

Recommended Textbooks for Tax Research

Basic U.S. Genealogical Records Group
Voter Records . . .

U.S. Voter Records	Voter Records Locations + What To Check
Board of Elections Lists	**Family Sources** .... *page 23*
Electoral Rolls	• Check for Biographical Info in Family Papers and Interviews
Political Affiliation	**Important U.S. Nat'l & State Gen. Libraries, Repos. & Archives** ...*24-26*
Voter Lists	• Check for State-level Voter Records
Voter Registration	**How to Find LOCAL Genealogical Repositories** *26-27*
	• Check County Clerk & Courthouse for Local-level Voter Records
	• Check for Local Newspaper and other public records
	Recommended Gen. Records/Resources Database Providers......*27-29*
	• Check for Voter Records, Biographical Sources, etc.
	Important U.S. Genealogical & Historical Societies............................*29*
	• Check for Local Voter Records and other record collections

Description of Voter Records
An interesting topic to add to your ancestor's biographical profile.

❧ **Voter Registration Records** are always worth checking since they may contain a birth date, occupation, whether convicted of a crime, length of residence, name change and possibly naturalization info. They may also give a residential address when other sources don't exist. They may be in card or computerized index form. To find your ancestor in the records, you'll need to know their state and city or town.

❧ **County & City Histories** can indicate a community's political views during your ancestor's day and often causes. When biographical sketches are included they can also give individuals' political affiliations.

❧ Some **City Directories** also included individuals' political affiliations.

❧ Search online and in local historical repositories for these **Political Organizations' Publications** since it was typical for them to publish lists of officers and members. They can also offer some historic context for your ancestors' lives by describing events, committees and causes.

❧ Current voter records are usually kept at the city or county level at the Board of Elections or similarly named office. Rarely do these offices house historic Voter Records (as most have either been moved or destroyed), so contact them for more information about their historic records.

Obtain Documents for Voter Records
❧ Check the Voter Records chart above. Pay special attention to the "**How To Find LOCAL Genealogical Repositories**" section (pages *26-27*).

Basic U.S. Genealogical Records Group
Wills & Probate Records . . .

U.S. Will / Probate Records	Will & Probate Records Locations + What To Check
Abstracted Wills	**Family Sources** .... *page 23*
Estate Settlements	• Check for Will & Probate Records in Family Papers and Interviews
Intestate Estate Records	**How to Find LOCAL Genealogical Repositories** 26-27
Newspaper Probate Notices	• Check County Clerk & Courthouse for Local Will & Probate Records
Probate Court's Minute Books	• Check for Local Newspaper and other public records
	Recommended Gen. Records/Resources Database Providers......27-29
Probate Records & Packets	• Check for Will & Probate Records, etc.
	Important U.S. Genealogical & Historical Societies............................29
	• Check for Local will & Probate Records and other record collections

Description of Wills & Probate Records
One of the most important genealogical records since they exist for all time periods of the U.S. and often identify family groups and their residences.
- 🦃 Will records are those <u>legal documents</u> created by the subject individual **before their death**, usually called A Last Will and Testament. Probate records are also <u>legal documents</u> created by the Probate Process of the courts to settle the estate **after the Testator's* death**, usually referred to as the Probate Packet. Both types of records are usually still located in the local Courthouse or Court Archive where they were originally filed, which was the Testator's place of residence at the time of death. Your goal should

---

* **Testator**: What the subject individual was called after death who had a Will to be put thru the court's Probate Process.

be to obtain both the Will and Probate Records since they usually contain information on then-current clusters of relatives, often those living near each other, sometimes biographical facts and typically clearly state the Testator's relationships to the people named.** They can also give unexpected information, like "previously unknown relatives or property." They are a type of records that were used during ALL time periods in U.S. history and are all typically located in court archives if still extant today. **The Probate Process:** 1) The Testator must have devised a Will before death which makes him Testate ("with a Will") as opposed to Intestate ("without a Will") . . . there may still be court proceedings for how to divide an estate even if there was no Will so it's best to check court records in either case. 2) A person involved with the Testator's estate brings the Will before the Probate Court (this person is typically named the Executor/Executrix or Administrator/ Administratrix). ***You may find records in the Probate Court's minutes books giving details plus executed documents in the Probate Packet stating who this person was.*** 3) The Probate Court "records the Will" usually with legal forms that are signed by the Executor. At this point in time, the Probate Court creates a Probate Packet for the case into which all of the documentation will be placed over the life of the proceedings. ***This is why you want to get the entire Probate Packet.*** 4) Since it is the Executor's job to make sure that all claims on the estate are paid before distributions can be made to the heirs, several things typically happened: a) The Executor placed a series of newspaper ads or other public notices in the Testator's residential location announcing that the estate was in probate and that any claims must be filed within a specified deadline. ***Check local newspapers for the probate notices***; b) The Executor pays any outstanding debts. ***This list is typically included in the Probate Packet.***; c) The Executor devised a List of Assets remaining in the estate. ***This list is typically included in the Probate Packet.***; d) Potential beneficiaries are contacted. ***Typically potential heirs' relationship to the Testator and their then-residency is included in the Probate Packet.*** 5) After the specified time has been met, the Executor submits all documents to the Probate Court. The estate is divided and distributed among the heirs. ***This list is typically included in the Probate Packet.*** The Will is now considered "fully proven" and the estate is settled. (A codicil or other legal instruments added to a Will may

---

** Since Will and Probate records often pass property from a parent to children (named as heirs and therefore the individuals' relationships to each other are clearly stated), Will and Probate records are widely used by genealogists as Parental Proof Evidence.

add further steps and documents to this process.)

🐿 In case of an Intestate Estate, you should search for all possible probate records in the court's paper packets/cases and any bound volume records regardless of the time period and location. Many states have statutes for the partition and distribution of real and personal estates.

Clues to Wills & Probate Information might be found:

Bibliographies, County Clerk's Records, Database Providers, Family Sources, Library Archives, Lineages on Social Media, Local Genealogical & Historical Societies, Newspapers-Death Notices & Obituaries, Religious Organizations, State Archives, State Department of Health Records, etc.

Obtain Documents for Wills & Probate Records

They are often still in the local Courthouse or Court Archives where they were originally filed. Indexes to these records can often be found online.

1. After identifying your ancestor's likely death location (and therefore likely Will/Probate records location), check indexes, etc. (as above), contact the local Courthouse or Court Archives. If the local repository is not obvious, find your ancestor's location on USGenWeb http://usgenweb.org/ or FamilySearch Wiki https://familysearch.org/wiki/

2. Remember your goal should be to obtain both the Will & Probate records (even if you've found an abstract or estate settlement).

🐿 Check the Wills & Probate Records chart above. See the "**How To Find LOCAL Genealogical Repositories**" section (pages *26-27*).

Recommended Guides To Will & Probate Research In General

Recommended Guides To Will & Probate Research In Their Collection

Recommended Textbooks for Will & Probate Research

SOME BASIC GENEALOGICAL TOOLS

For many more tools, see the textbook in this series, **Fundamentals of Genealogy®: The Most Helpful Tools You've Never Used**.

- 🌲 **Fundamentals of Genealogy® Ancestral Profile**.................Pages 7-8
- 🌲 **"Beginning Genealogy" Research Strategy**......................Appendix B
- 🌲 **"Brick Walls" Research Strategy** ....Appendix B
- 🌲 **"Conflicting Information" Research Strategy** ....Appendix B
- 🌲 **(U.S.) County Boundary Changes -** As the U.S. grew and changed so did the state and county boundaries. Since most governmental records were created in your ancestors' residential location at that time and were never moved, you need to know the name of the county then and whether the county boundaries changed. If so, you may need to look for records in two counties today. An easy way to determine the jurisdiction then and now is to use an interactive research tool like The Newberry Library's "Atlas of Historical County Boundaries" Interactive Map at www.newberry.org/ahcbp/.
- 🌲 **County Identifier** - RootsWeb's U.S Town/County Database .... at http://resources.rootsweb.ancestry.com/cgi-bin/townco.cgi
- 🌲 **Database Providers** – *"Recommended Gen. Records/Resources Database Providers" section*.. Pages 27-29
  - **Ancestry®** www.ancestry.com
  - **FamilySearch** https://familysearch.org
  - **FindAGrave** https://www.findagrave.com/
  - **Fold3** https://www.fold3.com
  - **Google Books** https://books.google.com
  - **HeritageQuest** (via public libraries) www.ancestryheritagequest.com
  - **MyHeritage** https://www.myheritage.com/
  - **NewspaperArchive** https://newspaperarchive.com/
  - **PERSI** (PERiodical Source Index) www.findmypast.com/persi
  - **RootsWeb** http://home.rootsweb.ancestry.com/
  - **Vital Rec** http://vitalrec.com/
  - **World Vital Records** (lib) www.worldvitalrecords.com/wvrhome.aspx
  - **WorldCat** www.worldcat.org/
- 🌲 **Education** – *"Recommended Educational Resources" section* 29-31
  - **Ancestry® Wiki** www.ancestry.com/wiki
  - **Board for the Certification of Genealogists' "Skillbuilding: Your Learning Center"** www.bcgcertification.org/skillbuilders/index.html
  - **BYU Family History Portal** http://familyhistory.byu.edu/
  - **Dear MYRTLE** http://blog.dearmyrtle.com/
  - **Eastman's Online Genealogy Newsletter** https://blog.eogn.com/

Fundamentals of Genealogy®: Basics for Everyone

Second edition, part of the *Fundamentals of Genealogy®* textbook series

- **FamilySearch Wiki** https://familysearch.org/wiki/en/Main_Page
- **Family Tree Magazine** www.familytreemagazine.com/
- **U.S. NARA** https://www.archives.gov/research/genealogy
- **U.S. National Genealogical Society** www.ngsgenealogy.org/
- **One-Step Webpages by Stephen P. Morse** www.stevemorse.org/
- **Rootsweb** http://home.rootsweb.ancestry.com/
- **ThoughtCo's Genealogy** https://www.thoughtco.com/genealogy-4133308

🎋 **Encyclopedia of Genealogy** .... http://eogen.editme.com

🎋 **Female Ancestors" Research Strategy** .... Appendix B

🎋 **"First Finding Sources" Research Strategy** .... Appendix B

🎋 **GEDCOM Digital File Format** .... *see the "Software" section*

🎋 **Google for genealogy -** Free **Google Account** https://www.Google.com
Many of Google's free features described below require that you set up a free account (if you're using Gmail you've already set one up --- simply Sign In with your established username and password).

- Genealogists often forget to do **Google searches for words and phrases *outside* of the most popular genealogy websites**. Before going to a databases, try a Google search instead using the tips below.
- **Maximize your Basic Google Searches** https://www.Google.com:
  - Use **"Search Operators"** along with the keywords/phrases https://support.google.com/websearch/answer/2466433?p=adv_operators&hl=en&rd=1
    ✓ Place a **phrase** within quotation marks to tell Google to search only for the exactly wording within the quotation marks, like "John Jacob Jingleheimer Schmidt"
    ✓ Make a dash the first character of a word to exclude from the search results. Use this with other **delimiters**, like –Reverend "Samuel Willard" (which indicates that you want results for Samuel Willard but not for the famous Reverend Samuel Willard).
    ✓ Try a little-used Proximity search using AROUND and NEAR as a delimiting wildcard. For AROUND: Used between two keywords such as a name, ***John AROUND(3) Smith***, asks for a maximum number of 3 keywords with ***John*** proceeding ***Smith*** and any word before, between or after (results included ***Captain John Smith***, ***John Maynard Smith*** and ***John Smith I***). For NEAR: Used between two keywords such as a name, ***John NEAR Smith***, asks for three words in any order with ***John*** and ***Smith*** required (results included ***John Smith***, ***John Smith's Beach*** and ***St. John's Smith Square***).
- **Google Advanced Search** https://www.google.com/advanced_search
  - Use **"last update"** for the most recent webpage additions.

Page 70   **_Fundamentals of Genealogy®_ textbook series**   © 2017, Marsha Peterson-Maass

- Use **"site or domain"** to search within one website (or in a normal Google search, use "site:SITEURL" before the term)
- Use **"terms appearing"** to limit search results and find them for "in the title of the page," "in the URL" and more.
- At the **bottom of this screen** "Find pages that are similar to a URL," "Search pages you've visited" "Use operators in the search box" and "Customize your search settings."
- Find **YouTube videos** https://www.YouTube.com about using Google by searching with simple keywords like "Google genealogy."
- *For more Google tips, see **Fundamentals of Genealogy®: The Most Helpful Tools You've Never Used** textbook.*

🌿 **Handwriting/Paleography Tools** - FamilySearch's **"Handwriting Helps"** https://familysearch.org/indexing/help/handwriting#!/lang=en&title=Alphabet%20(Secretary%20Hand) "Whether you are struggling to read old handwriting or working in an unfamiliar language, we have resources to help you!"

- **Expect inconsistencies in handwriting** even in the same document.
- Online guide for **Letter Examination** (general public) www.business balls.com/graphologytest.pdf
- Online guide for **Personality Thru Handwriting Analysis**: www.ehow.com - search "Basics of Handwriting Analysis"
- **Paleography video** https://youtu.be/oQVZfQRXLjo
- Other handwriting questions? You're sure to find some answers in the following **CyndisList** "Handwriting & Script >> Professionals" www.cyndis list.com/handwriting/professionals/ and "Handwriting & Script >> Professionals" www.cyndislist.com/handwriting/general/

🌿 **Heraldry** – CyndisList ...www.cyndislist.com/cyndislistsearch/?q=heraldry

- Allen County Public Library Genealogy Center's "Heraldry" Pathfinder .www.genealogycenter.org/Pathfinders/Guides/Heraldry.aspx
- International Register of Arms .... www.armorial-register.com/

🌿 **Hiring a Professional Genealogist**

- **Association of Professional Genealogists** ..https://www.apgen.org/
- **Board for Certification of Genealogists**.... www.bcgcertification.org/
- **CyndisList–Prof'l Researchers** ...... www.cyndislist.com/professionals
- **DNA Finding U** (Genetic Genealogy) .... www.dnafindingu.com
- **Council for Adv. Forensic Genealogy** www.forensicgenealogists.org/

🌿 **History (Local History)** – *These websites have made it easy for you to put our ancestors in their historical context.*

- **Histography** http://histography.io ". . . draws on Wikipedia entries to picture the past on animated timelines."

- **HistoryLines** https://historylines.com/ (subscription) instant family history by creating ancestral stories that place your ancestor in their historic context.
- **HistoryPin** https://www.historypin.org/en/ "Connecting communities with local history" by collaborating with pinners (individuals, archives, libraries, museums, etc.) that contribute historical photos plotted on Google maps and matched to modern street views.

🪶 **Maps and Gazetteers -** *Maps are a wonderful genealogical tool for so many things . . . placing our ancestors in their historic context . . . giving us clues to possible locations of relatives, ethnic neighborhoods, education, worship, employment, etc. Make sure you're not infringing on any copyrights when using maps (know that maps directly from the U.S. federal government are copyright free).*

- **The David Rumsey Map Collection** www.davidrumsey.com
- Find **popular genealogical gazetteers** with a Google search using the keyword "gazetteer" + location names.
- **U.S. Geological Survey (USGS)** https://www.usgs.gov/ **and USGS Library** http://library.usgs.gov/
- **Hargrett's Historical Maps** and **Historical Maps Database** www.libs.uga.edu/hargrett/maps/index.html
- **Library of Congress: Maps** https://www.loc.gov/maps/collections/
- **Library of Congress: Geography & Map Division** http://www.loc.gov/rr/geogmap/gmpage.html
- **(U.S.) National Archives and Records Administration's Maps** https://www.archives.gov/research/maps
- **(U.S.) National Atlas of the United States** https://www.data.gov/ search for specific maps on the Home Page.
- **Newberry Library's "Maps, Travel and Exploration"** https://www.newberry.org/maps-travel-and-exploration
- **JewishGen's Shtetl Seeker** www.jewishgen.org/ShtetlSeeker

🪶 **Notetaking Software Systems (Evernote and OneNote) -**

- **Evernote** https://evernote.com is a free (and paid upgradable) organizational digital notetaking system for both Windows and Mac that allows you to capture computer screen shots in two clicks, makes instant image files, is searchable and sharable with other users. You can even sync it to your digital devices when connected to the Cloud.
  - Find Evernote video tutorials on YouTube https://www.youtube.com by searching keywords "Evernote," "Tutorial" and "Genealogy."
  - The **Evernote Apps Center** is at https://appcenter.evernote.com/
  - **"Making the Move from Evernote to OneNote"** (with the OneNote Importer) www.onenote.com/import-evernote-to-onenote
- **OneNote** www.onenote.com/ is an organizational digital notetaking system for Windows that is part of the Office 365 Suite. It does the same tasks as outlined in Evernote above.
- **"Notetaking Software-For Search" Research Strategy** .... Appendix B
- **"Notetaking Software-Template" Research Strategy** .... Appendix B
- **One-Step Webpages by Stephen P. Morse** www.stevemorse.org/ Use Steve's one-step portal to search websites for records relating to "Ellis Island, Castle Garden and Other Ports," "U.S. Census," "Phonetic Matching," "UK / Canada Census," "New York Census," "Vital Records," "Calendar, Maps, etc.," "Foreign Alphabets" and much more.
- **PERSI (the PERiodical Source Index)** www.findmypast.com/persi - Is a FREE searchable index of nearly 3 million genealogical journal entries for articles from +8,000 international but primarily U.S.-based national and local genealogical, historical and ethnic periodicals. It's consistently updated by the Allen County (IN) Public Library (so remember to keep checking it often). Since PERSI is searchable by article titles (not always including a family surname in that title), you can find many family history entries by using these search tips:
  - **"Subject":** Search for a family group in the "Subject" entry line by using the surname and location (the most narrows as possible), knowing that you may not receive the best results unless you have an unusual surname or location. Reviewing the "Periodical" results column will give you ideas for possible periodical sources to check in a different search.
  - **"Town/City," "County" and "State":** Search for a family group at a time by identifying which periodicals might include information on them based on their residential location during a range of time. You might have better luck with smaller, local publications than with state or national publications. Start your search in the "Town/City" entry line, then try the "State" and "County" entry lines.
  - **"Article Keyword" and "Optional Keywords":** Think of the aspects

of your ancestors' live that may have appeared in local or specialty periodical articles . . . family reunions, anniversaries, religious activities, social activism, etc. Use the "Keywords" entry lines by themselves or in combination with other entry lines.

- **"How-To Article":** Use the "How-To Article" entry line for just about any kind of specialized Help article you need, especially when you're newly researching in local sources you're unfamiliar with.
- Once you've found a pertinent entry in PERSI, how do you obtain the original periodical article? Two ways: 1) Get it thru PERSI by clicking on that icon at the right of the results line, or; 2) PERSI gives you the source citation information, so either locate the specific periodical at a local library or locate it in OCLC (search http://www.worldcat.org/) and see whether you can order it thru Inter-Library Loan.
- Find more information about PERSI in the FamilySearch Wiki at https://familysearch.org/wiki/en/Periodical_Source_Index_(PERSI)

- "**Relationship**"........www.cyndislist.com/cyndislistsearch/?q=relationship
- **Relationship Terms From The Past**
  - **"Brother"** and **"Sister"** – could refer to a religious association.
  - **"Cousin"** – any familial relationship other than parents and children. Nieces and nephews were often referred to as cousins.
  - **"His Now Wife"** – not "a second wife," instead a legal term to protect an estate from other claimants pretending to have property rights.
  - **"Nepos"** – Latin for "Grandson," not an abbreviation for nephew.
  - **"Senior"** and **"Junior"** – could refer to two men with the same name in the same location, the elder is "Senior," with or without a blood tie.
  - **"Sister"** – could mean a sister or sister-in-law.
  - *CyndisList* www.cyndislist.com/cyndislistsearch/?q=relationship%20terms

- **U.S. Social Security Records:**
  - **U.S. Social Security Death Index** ("SSDI") was first compiled in 1962. When people who were receiving U.S. Social Security payments passed away, they and several pieces of their information were added to this list – Name, SS#, Birth Date, Death Date, Residence City, Where Last Check Mailed and State Applied In. This index is currently available at several websites including FamilySearch.org "United States

Social Security Death Index" https://familysearch.org/search/collection/1202535?collection NameFilter=true and Ancestry.com (this database records collection is called, "U.S., Social Security Death Index, 1936-2014").

- **U.S. Social Security Applications and Claims Index** is a relatively new index that is similar to the SSDI (see above) but offers a bit more information online, including Parents' Names (with mother's maiden name) and Subject's Subsequent Names and other information in the notes section. This index is currently available at Ancestry.com entitled, "U.S., Social Security Applications and Claims Index, 1936-2007".
- **SS-5 Form** is the original card ancestors completed to receive a U.S. Social Security number. Registrations began after Congress passed the "Social Security Act" in 1935. You can order a photocopy of the original card thru a Freedom of Information Act Request at the U.S. Social Security Administration's website https://www.ssa.gov/foia/request.html
- Order **other Social Security records**, like for those individuals not listed in the SSDI (who died before 1962), directly from the U.S. Social Security Administration with details at https://www.ssa.gov/foia/request.html

- 🌿 **Societies** – *"Important U.S. Genealogical & Historical Societies"* . Page 29
  - **FamilySearch.org Wiki** https://familysearch.org/wiki/
  - **Federation of Genealogical Societies** ("FGS") http://fgs.org/
  - **National Genealogical Society** ("NGS") www.ngsgenealogy.org
  - **Obituary Links Page** – listed by state www.obitlinkspage.com/hs/
  - **YouTube** www.YouTube.com search for organizations' channels
- 🌿 **"Surname Meanings & Origins"** from ThoughtCo ....
  https://www.thoughtco.com/surname-meanings-and-origins-s2-1422408
- 🌿 **Translation Tools -** For English speakers, when researching ancestors who spoke another language, use **search terms both in English and in their language**. For language reference help, use translation tools at CyndisList and FamilySearch Wiki.
  - CyndisList **"Languages & Translation"** www.cyndislist.com/languages/
  - CyndisList's **"Translation Services"** offer unique suggestions for your genealogical translation questions, some free, some require hiring an expert www.cyndislist.com/cyndislistsearch/?q=translation
  - FamilySearch Wiki's **Latin words/terms**, "Latin Genealogical Word List" https://familysearch.org/wiki/en/Latin Genealogical Word List

BASIC GENEALOGICAL ANALYSIS, RECORDING, ORGANIZATION & NETWORKING TECHNIQUES

Genealogical Analysis Process, Guidelines And Formatting Basics . . .

The Analysis Process consists of the outlined components below. Once you are familiar with these accredited standards, you'll be able to quickly evaluate the quality of proof from the evidence you've found, helping you to formulate a research plan which should include an exhaustive search (part of GPS).

Checklist For The Genealogical Analysis Process
Today, the accepted **Standard of Proof** is based on "proof by clear and convincing evidence" and "valuing sources based on their analyzed weight." *For a detailed treatment of proof, see the book **Mastering Genealogical Proof** in the "**Bibliography**" section.*

Follow this outline of components of the **Genealogical Analysis Process** as part of the **"#4-Accredited Research and Planning Process"** (part #4 on the "Checklist – *Fundamentals of Genealogy*® Start With Accredited Methods," page 4):
• **"Standard of Proof"** (above)
• **"*Fundamentals of Genealogy®: Analysis Style Sheet*"** (77-78)
    • **"Evidence Evaluation & Weighing To Substantiate Proof Process"** (pages 77-78)
        →→→ **"Weighing The Evidence Analysis Process"**
    • **"The 5-Step Genealogical Proof Standard"** (page 78)
        →→→ How to integrate the GPS steps in to your genealogy project
• **Use a Timeline** – see Appendix B: *Fundamentals of Genealogy*® Research Strategy, **"Brick Walls – Strategies For Breaking Thru"** (page 101) and **"Notetaking Software – A Format To Quicken, Organize And Record Your Research"** (page 105)
• **Planning including Research Strategies** (pages 100-106)
    • **"Conflicting Information** - How Do I Resolve It?" (page 102)
    • **"Brick Walls** – Strategies For Breaking Thru" (page 101)
    • **"Notetaking Software** – A Format To Quicken, Organize And Record Your Research"** (page 105)

Follow up your initial analysis work with: • *See the **"Networking"** section* (pages 88-92)

Fundamentals of Genealogy® Analysis Style Sheet

Every time you find genealogical info, put it thru the **"Evidence Evaluation & Weighing To Substantiate Proof Process"**	
Stage	**Component Process**
Stage 1: Source	Determine the **Source** that supplied the information. →→→ Record a proper Source Citation . . . *see the "Recording" section.*
Stage 2: Information	Determine the Information that the **Source** supplied. →→→ Record the Information . . . *see the "Recording" section.*

Stage 3: "Weighing The Evidence" Analysis Process	Determine its **Weight As Evidence** (to substantiate reliability, credibility & relevance) →→→ Put it thru the **"Weighing The Evidence Analysis Process"** below:
	 1. Original vs. Derivative Concept . . .
	     Original = A source initially recorded to contribute information of a circumstance/event.
	     Derivative = A source that is not the Original but contributes information abstracted, duplicated, transcribed or otherwise taken from a previously existing source.
	 This Concept = Traditionally, the Original carries most weight. Always try to get the original or as close a copy to the original as possible.
	 2. Primary Event Knowledge vs. Secondary Event Knowledge Concept . . .
	     Primary Event Knowledge = A source person who was an eyewitness to the event.
	     Secondary Event Knowledge = A source person who was not an eyewitness.
	 This Concept = The Primary Event Knowledge can carry most weight if the informant and recorder of the information are credible sources.
	 3. Primary Relationship Reliability vs. Secondary Relationship Reliability Concept . . .
	     Primary Relationship Reliability = A source person who had close personal knowledge of the individual(s) for whom he/she provided information.
	     Secondary Relationship Reliability = A source person lacking personal knowledge.
	 This Concept = Primary Relationship Reliability carries most weight if credible informant.
	 4. Direct Evidence vs. Indirect Evidence Concept . . .
	     Direct Evidence = When the evidence appears to answer the question explicitly and does not require support or amplification from another source (although supporting evidence from independent sources would still be highly desirable, since the fact that the information directly answers the question still does not mean it is accurate).
	     Indirect Evidence = When the evidence appears to be relevant to the question, but it does not answer the question explicitly and it needs additional evidence to support or correct it before a conclusion can be reached.
	 This Concept = Each type is important; the credibility of the record or source can help determine the analytical weight.
	 5. Primary Source vs. Secondary Source Concept . . .
	     Primary Source = A Primary Source is information that was documented by an eyewitness at or close to the time of the event. Also known as "Best Evidence" since it produces the highest possible degree of proof due to its source. An original source or record would be considered Primary Evidence.
	     Secondary Source = A Secondary Source is information that was documented a while after the event possibly by someone who was or wasn't an eyewitness to the event.
	 This Concept = Genealogists typically give more weight to Primary Sources. Both are important to a body of evidence.

Fundamentals of Genealogy® Analysis Style Sheet

Stage 4: Fact	Determine whether this Evidence has been found to **Possess Truth**. →→→ Ask, "Does this Evidence possess truth?" If "Yes," continue to Step 5.
Stage 5: Proof Summary	Sum up the Opinion of all measurable analyses for this **Fact**. →→→ Put together a **Proof Summary** of all measurable analyses in Steps 1-4.

An example, starting with a Question *–* *"What is Carrie's birth date?"*

Stage 1 →→→ **Source Citation:** (Woods) Tull Scott, Caroline. Standard Certificate of Death (uncertified photocopy), 18 May 1934. County Clerk's Office, Hancock County, Illinois, U.S.A.

Stage 2 →→→ **Information**: Carrie's birth date was "10 November 1845."

Stage 3 →→→ **"Weighing The Evidence Analysis Process":** It appears to carry strong weight.
- **Original Record** *(a government issued Death Certificate)*
- **Secondary Event Knowledge** *(informant was her son who was not present at her birth)*
- **Primary Relationship Reliability** *(information was her son who lived with her)*
- **Direct Evidence** *(the information directly answers the question)*
- **Secondary Source Record** *(the information was recorded a long time after her birth)*

Stage 4 →→→ **Fact**: This has been substantiated as a fact since the evidence possesses truth.

Stage 5 →→→ **Proof Summary**: "Our research produced a vital record [*government issued death certificate*] that states Carrie's birth date was 10 November 1845. This Information can be considered Evidence since it is relevant to the question at hand. Our Weighed Evidence appears to carry strong weight [*Original Record-Death Certificate + Secondary Event Knowledge-Son was not present at Carrie's birth + Primary Relationship Reliability-Son lived with Carrie + Direct Evidence-It answers the question + a Secondary Source Record-Recorded a long time after Carrie's birth*]."

When you need to resolve conflicting info or want to confirm your accurate family history, put it thru the **"The 5-Step Genealogical Proof Standard"** *

GPS Step	Process Explanation
GPS-Step One:	<u>Reasonably exhaustive search.</u> "We conduct a reasonably exhaustive search for all information that is or may be pertinent to the identity, relationship, event or situation in question" . . . *see Fundamentals of Genealogy®* Checklist - Start With Accredited Methods ***"#4-Research"*** *(pages3-4) and "Research Strategy -* ***Brick Walls"*** *(page 101)*
GPS-Step Two:	<u>Complete an accurate citation of sources.</u> "We collect and include in our compilation a complete, accurate citation to the source or sources of each item of information we use" . . .*see "Recording." (pages 79-81)*
GPS-Step Three:	<u>Analysis and correlation of the collected information.</u> "We analyze and correlate the collected information to assess its quality as evidence" . . .*see* ***"Evidence Evaluation & Weighing To Substantiate Proof Process"*** *(above).*
GPS-Step Four: *(when you have conflicting info)*	<u>Resolution of conflicting evidence.</u> "We resolve any conflicts caused by items of evidence that contradict each other or are contrary to a proposed (hypothetical) solution to the question" . . .*see* **Research Strategy *"Conflicting Information - How Do I Resolve It?"*** *(page 102).*
GPS-Step Five:	<u>Soundly reasoned, coherently written conclusion.</u> "We arrive at a soundly reasoned, coherently written conclusion" . . .*see the "Recording" section. (pages 79-81)*

* From Thomas W. Jones' book *Mastering Genealogical Proof (*National Genealogical Society, Arlington, VA, 2013).
** Information taken from *The BCG Genealogical Standards Manual* (Washington, D.C.: Board for Certification, 2014), pp. 1-2; also find it on The Board for Certification of Genealogists' website www.bcgcertification.org.

Genealogical Recording Guidelines and Formatting Basics . . .

- **How To Record Information In A Family Tree Or Chart**
  - Enter individuals' names at birth . . . *see the **Recording Style Sheet**.*
  - For a married couple, Male in left box, a double horizontal line connects the boxes and Female in the right box . . . *see **Ancestral Fan Chart**.*
  - Enter surnames either in all caps or first letter capitalized (most software programs will allow you to convert this in a few clicks).
  - For your digital and online family tree, create only ONE large family tree so you can create charts and reports that include everyone.
  - For more info and forms, see FamilySearch's "**Genealogy Research Forms**" https://familysearch.org/wiki/en/Genealogy_Research_Forms
  - See CyndisList "**Beginners >> Beginners Guides, Hints & Tips**" http://www.cyndislist.com/beginners/beginners-guides-hints-and-tips/
  - Find more suggestions in the textbook, ***Fundamentals of Genealogy®: The Most Helpful Tools You've Never Used.***
- **Extract** = To take out "a portion" of another source "word for word."
- **Abstract** = To re-word the meaning of another source.
- **Transcription** = A literal "word for word" derivative of an entire source.
- **Translation** = To convert one language to another.
- **Source Citations** – General formats for genealogical records:
  - **Bibliography [unauthored records]:**
    Country. County. State. City. Organization name. Source title.
  - **Bibliography [authored works]:**
    Surname, First name. "Article's title." Publication name. Vol. #, Date.
  - **Footnote or Endnote [unauthored records]:**
    1. Source title: Entry title and/or Page #. Organization name, Physical location including city, county, state, country.
  - **Footnote or Endnote [authored works]:**
    1. First name and Surname, "Article's title," Publication name, Vol. # (Date). Comments like where the record begins.
- **Source Citations** – What **UNUSUAL** info to include for these records:
  - **U.S. Federal Census** – 1) Online organization's image #, 2) URL, 3) Physical location, 4) NARA microfilm roll and page #, 5) NARA location.
  - **Cemetery Record** – 1) Physical location and plot #, 2) If book transcription, 3) If a visit or site photo, 4) Date and source of info.
  - **Newspaper Record** – 1) Microfilm roll #, 2) Location of provider, 3) Original newspaper source info, image and page #, 4) URL, 5) Online organization's physical location.
  - **Vital Records** – 1) Organization physical location, 2) Record #, 3) If microfilm, Roll #, 4) Location provider, 5) If online, online organization's image # or URL, organization's physical location.

Fundamentals of Genealogy® Recording Style Sheet

Genealogical Recording Format Basics

COMMENTS

- **Genealogist's Comments:** Use square brackets when adding a comment, for example [my comment clarifying a date goes here].

NAMES

- **Surnames:** Some genealogists capitalize every letter of a SURNAME. A software database allows you to transpose in a few clicks.
- **Female Name:** Given Middle (Maiden Surname) Married Surname
- **Female Name with Nickname:** Given Middle "Nickname" (Maiden Surname) Married Surname(s) in order of marriages

ENTERING NAMES INTO DATABASE SOFTWARE PROGRAM

- **Names at Birth:** Enter your ancestors' names at birth, females' names are listed at their maiden name.
- **Names in Foreign Language:** Choose how you will display your ancestors' names, input the primary choice in their profile main naming fields, then input the secondary choice in the "A/K/A naming field" (meaning "Also Known As").

ENTERING NAMES INTO AN ONLINE DATABASE

- Use the guidelines above. If no A/K/A field, use the name at birth.

LOCATIONS

- **Urban Locations:** Street Address, Apartment, Ward at the time, Township, County/Parish, State, U.S.A.
- **Rural Locations:** Street Address, Community Name, Land Section #, Township, County/Parish, State, U.S.A.

DATES

- **Date Format:** Write dates in this format, "24 January 1905."
- **Transcribing Dates:** If the U.S. date on the original is "7/8/47" then record it as "7/8/47 [08 July 1847]."

___

Summary of Genealogical Software and Why It's So Important . . .

Many of today's genealogists are choosing an integrated approach to digitally record, organize and store much of their genealogical information . . . using an online database provider like Ancestry® that syncs with software that also resides on your Windows or Mac computing devices . . . this approach offers us software options for printing charts and reports that those online database providers don't currently offer. But which genealogical software is right for you? The answer lies in the means of your initial recording of the genealogical information (or syncing) and your goals for the final output, like charts and reports. Many genealogists who subscribe to Ancestry® use Family Tree Maker® software on their electronic devices that has FamilySync along with the ability to generate charts and reports beyond what Ancestry® offers.

🌿 Genealogical Software Recommendations

- **GenSoft Reviews!** www.gensoftreviews.com/index.php currently the most comprehensive website with software reviews. Don't forget to click the "See Program Rankings" and "See Award Winners" links.
- For more ideas, go to **Pinterest** www.Pinterest.com and search on keywords, like "genealogy" and "software."
- CyndisList "**Software**" www.cyndislist.com/cyndislistsearch/?q=software
- **Genealogy Apps** - Check your software's website for downloadable apps that can sync your electronic devices and online-based program.
- Find more "**Software for genealogy**" suggestions in *Fundamentals of Genealogy®: The Most Helpful Tools You've Never Used*.

🌿 Getting Help With Genealogical Software

- If trying the software's own "Help" section isn't enough, search **CyndisList** www.cyndislist.com/ with the software name.
- Check **Facebook** https://www.facebook.com/ for user groups.
- For more ideas, go to **Pinterest** www.Pinterest.com and search on keywords, like "genealogy" and "software," then "help."

🌿 GEDCOM Digital File Format

- A GEDCOM digital file is a **standardized file format** that genealogical software can read so you can share files between different programs.
- CyndisList "**GEDCOM**" www.cyndislist.com/cyndislistsearch/?q=gedcom
- **GEDCOM-to-Webpage Conversion Software**, see CyndsList page www.cyndislist.com/gedcom/gedcom-to-web-page-conversion/
- For **YouTube** www.YouTube.com instructional videos, search with keywords like "GEDCOM," and "genealogical software."

___

"The *Fundamentals of Genealogy®* Organizational Challenge" . . .

How is the Fundamentals of Genealogy® Organizational Challenge different than other organizational systems? We'll tackle your current "unorganized circumstance" ONE TASK at a time, then we'll maintain your organization within a Project Management System Framework! See **Fundamentals of Genealogy®: The Most Helpful Tools You've Never Used.**

#1-PREP WITHIN A FRAMEWORK - clean up & maintain organization

If you start with this prep, the clean-up and maintenance items immediately have a place to go within your organized system.

- 🌿 **Prep To Clean Up -** Establish a place and organizational system for the paper, digital items, heirlooms, etc. . . *see the following Style Sheet.*
- 🌿 **Prep To Maintain -** Establish a place and organizational system for the paper, digital items, heirlooms, etc. . . *see the following Style Sheet.*
- 🌿 **Prep By Knowing Where To Get Education & Help –** Learn about organizational options that work for you and know where to seek help. Here are some recommendations:
  - Drew Smith's textbook, **Organize Your Genealogy: Strategies and Solutions for Every Researcher** (copyright and published in 2016, Family Tree Books, Cincinnati, Ohio)
  - Lisa Louise Cooke's webinar, **"Organize Your Online Genealogy Life"** http://familytreewebinars.com/download.php?webinar_id=369
  - Denise May Levenick (The Family Curator)'s textbook, **How to Archive Family Keepsakes: Learn how to preserve family photos, memorabilia & Genealogy records** (copyright and published in 2014, Family Tree Books, Cincinnati, Ohio)
  - **The Organized Genealogist Facebook Group** from DearMYRTLE and friends https://www.facebook.com/groups/organizedgenealogist/
  - **Organizing Your Family History blog** by Janine Adams http://organizeyourfamilyhistory.com/
  - **FamilySearch Wiki "Organizing Your Files"** https://familysearch.org/wiki/en/Organizing_Your_Files
  - Family Tree Magazine's article, **"Family Tree Tips: 23 Tips to Organize Your Genealogy"** http://www.familytreemagazine.com/family-tree-tips-23-secrets-to-organize-your-genealogy
  - Find instructional videos on **YouTube** www.YouTube.com searching with keywords like "genealogy organization."
  - See **CyndisList's** many categories covering Organizational topics at www.cyndislist.com/cyndislistsearch/?q=organize

Fundamentals of Genealogy® Organizational Challenge Style Sheet

Organizational System Summarizing the <u>Location</u> of your Paper + Digital Items		
Location	**Storage Device (for paper)**	**Contents**
Paper		
•		
•		
•		
•		
•		
•		
•		
•		
•		
•		
•		
•		
Digital and Online		
•		
•		
•		
•		
•		
•		
•		
•		
•		
•		
•		

<u>Sticky Notes Keywords</u>:
1) **Scan**---Type of scan and stored where? "**PDF**" or "**JPG**" or "**Doc**" + **Location Stored**
2) **Info**---Add this record's info where? "**Ancestral Software**" or "**Online Account**," etc.
3) **Citation**---If not recorded on the paper itself, put it here. "**Citation**"
4) **Inventory**---Added to your inventory of records yet? "**Inventory**"
5) **Paper**---Paper stored (chart above)? "**Shred**" or "**Bookshelf 3-ring Binder**," etc.

Fundamentals of Genealogy® Organizational Challenge Style Sheet

Make an Inventory of the Paper + Digital Items to Organize

Item to Organize	Storage Selection Type			
	Archival	Active	Reference	Purgeable
	Archival	Active	Reference	Purgeable
	Archival	Active	Reference	Purgeable
	Archival	Active	Reference	Purgeable
	Archival	Active	Reference	Purgeable
	Archival	Active	Reference	Purgeable
	Archival	Active	Reference	Purgeable
	Archival	Active	Reference	Purgeable
	Archival	Active	Reference	Purgeable
	Archival	Active	Reference	Purgeable
	Archival	Active	Reference	Purgeable
	Archival	Active	Reference	Purgeable
	Archival	Active	Reference	Purgeable
	Archival	Active	Reference	Purgeable
	Archival	Active	Reference	Purgeable
	Archival	Active	Reference	Purgeable

Create a digital "Tree" folder in your computer filing system. Within it create subfolders like these and place your digital files inside.

_Client-Hodek [*for current projects, like client work or lineage society memberships, etc.*]
0140-McFarland [*for family group information based on a direct ancestor's fan chart #*]
Census Images [*add subfolders by year with a Word document master listing for ancestors*]
Charts and Forms [*including GEDCOM files*]
Correspondence [*or place these digitized items in Evernote / OneNote instead*]
Log-Research Notes [*or place these items in Evernote / OneNote instead*]
Photos [*with a Word document master listing for ancestors*]
x_Czech [*for generic ethnic-specific information*]
y_Military-Civil War [*for generic record type-specific information*]
z_USA-Illinois-Adams County [*for generic location-specific information*]

→ Notice that there is no **"Miscellaneous"** subfolder. ←

Create digital file names using Source Citation information.

PROBATE_NOTICE-Jones_John-Quincy_Daily_Herald-26April1889-p3 [*in "00064-Jones" folder*]
1880-IL-Adams-Ursa-Roll_T9_174-FamilyHistoryFilm1254174_p1 [*in the "Census Images" folder*]
Collection_Guide_2016-Swedish_American_Museum_Chicago [*in the "x_Swedish" folder*]

- **An example** of how to fill in the Organizational System Style Sheet.

Organizational System Summarizing the <u>Location</u> of your Paper + Digital Items		
Location	**Storage Device (paper)**	**Contents**
Paper		
• Bookshelf-Office	3-ring binders	Copies of Vital Records
• Bookshelf-Office	Accordion file folders	Family Files
• Attic	Large airtight plastic bins	Family Memorabilia
Digital and Online		
• Family Tree GEDCOMs	C:\Tree\GEDCOMs	
• Scanned Vital Records	C:\Tree\VitalRecords	
• Scanned Family Files	C:\Tree\002-Peterson	
• Scanned Family Memorabilia	C:\Tree\002-Peterson\Memorabilia	

So how are you able to fill in the blank Organizational Style Sheet chart? Follow the four underlined steps below.

- **First, make an inventory of the items to organize.** On this example chart, circle whether they're Archival, Active, Reference or Purgeable:
  "<u>Archival</u>" = Materials that are usually heirlooms, keepsakes and information worth preserving.
    These are usually stored in large, airtight, sunlight and moisture-resistant plastic storage bins.
  "<u>Active</u>" = Materials that are usually found records that need to be recorded and scanned.
    These are usually stored nearby for immediate use, like in 3-ring binders and accordion files.
  "<u>Reference</u>" = Materials that help in research or other future activities.
    These are usually stored in accessible places, like books on bookshelves or files in drawers.
  "<u>Purgeable</u>" = Helpful until recorded or saved in digital form, like paper research notes + periodicals.
    These are usually digitized (or not), then donated to charity or shredded or otherwise eliminated.

Make an Inventory of the Paper + Digital Items to Organize				
Item to Organize	**Storage Selection Type**			
Family Letters, Postcards, etc. - Paper	Archival	Active	Reference	Purgeable
Heirlooms	Archival	Active	Reference	Purgeable
Periodicals	Archival	Active	Reference	Purgeable
Photos of family - Paper	Archival	Active	Reference	Purgeable
Records - Paper	Archival	Active	Reference	Purgeable

- Make an **inventory of family photos** as well!
- **Some basic organizational recommendations:**
  - ✓ Assign an Accordion file folder to your Family Groups.
  - ✓ Place the paper files you use most in 3-ring binders close to you.
  - ✓ Use as few sub-folders as possible, for both paper and digital files.
- **<u>Second</u>, make an inventory of the paper storage devices you already have.** Read some of the recommended "Education and Help"

items (above). Then note the other paper storage devices you want to purchase and add them to your inventory. Store paper in devices that will protect from the natural elements – airtight, sunlight resistant, moisture resistant, etc. – *see the "Preservation" section.*
- **Shelves** for most used paper items.
- **Drawers with Hanging Files** for generic info you use often, like paper maps or ethnic guides.
- **Accordion Files** for Family Group paper items.
- **Bin Storage** for keepsakes and paper items you don't regularly use.
- Plan on using a Scanner of some sort, whether you have a traditional scanner with your computer, or take papers to a Copying & Printing Service (like FedEx Office) or HIGHLY RECOMMENDED turn your smartphone into a scanner with an app like **Cam Scanner** https://www.camscanner.com/ . . . *see "Scanning The Paper Is Essential" in the "Basic Genealogical Tools" section.*
- **Third, for your future paper,** if you don't have time to deal with the PAPER RECORDS YOU ACQUIRE AS SOON AS YOU GET THEM, all of the future paper goes in to protective sleeves in your new "Genealogical In-Box." Place a sticky note on the outside of the protective plastic sleeve where you write a few keywords detailing how you will put that paper record into your system when you have time . . . *see the "Style Sheet."*
- **Four, you'll organize your digital files in Framework #2.**

#2 CLEAN-UP AND MAINTENANCE WITHIN A FRAMEWORK
Now that you've got a place and organizational system for your current and future items, let's go tackle the mess and keep it organized.

- **"INITIATING" --- Organizational Challenge Process #1**
  - Refer to your prep work on the "Organizational System Summary" chart you filled in on the Organizational Challenge Style Sheet.
- **"PLANNING" --- Organizational Challenge Process #2**
  - On your calendar, schedule "an appointment" for at least 1 hour to work on organizing your genealogy. Don't accept interruptions. Once you're done with that hour, schedule another and reward yourself!
  - Can you schedule an hour a day? Or an hour a week? Whatever works!
- **"EXECUTING" --- Organizational Challenge Process #3**
  - **For Paper Clean-Up**, organize one pile of paper at a time using the "Organizational System Summary" chart you filled in on the Organizational Challenge Style Sheet.
  - As you are organizing your Records, add them to your "Records Inventory" spreadsheet so you know where you have stored them.

Fundamentals of Genealogy® **Records Inventory** (Direct Ancestors listed by their Ancestral Fan Chart #) © 2017, Fundamentals of Genealogy®	Birth Records	Marriage Records	Divorce Records	Death Records	Baptismal Records	Religious Records	Cemetery Records	Tombstone Inscription	Obituaries	Newspaper Records	Census Records	Land Records	Migration Records	Social Security Records	Wills & Probate Records	Court Records	Military Personnel File	Military Pension File	Military Muster List	Military Misc. Records	Naturalization Records	Immigration Records	Family Records	Biographical Records	Directory Records	Tax Records	Ethnic Records	Educational Records	Employment Records	Club Records	Medical Records	Bible Records	Other
#001 Your Name Here (You)																																	
#002 Your Father's Name Here (Your Father)																																	
#003 Your Mother's Name Here (Your Mother)																																	

In this Word document, enter information by placing your cursor in the corresponding cell, choosing "References >> Insert Footnote" which places a number in the cell and opens a footnote text box at the bottom of the page for you to enter → **Citation info + location** where the paper & digital files are stored in your organized system.

- **For Digital Clean-Up**, set up a new computer filing structure (*see the Organizational Style Sheet*), having many broad folders and individual family group folders (beginning with the Ancestral Fan Chart file #).
- **For Digital File Names**, place as much source citation info in the digital file name as possible (we always want the citation to be attached to the record in some form). *See the Organizational Style Sheet.*

❧ "MONITORING & CONTROLLING" --- Organizational Challenge Process #4

- Maintain the process of putting paper records in your new "Genealogical In-box" when you don't have time to immediately add them to your organized system. Schedule time regularly to add them, using your "Organizational System Summary" chart as your guide.
- Can you commit to doing this Organizational Challenge annually? Can you make it your New Year's Resolution every year?

❧ "LATHER-RINSE-REPEAT" --- Organizational Challenge Process #5

- Lather, rinse, repeat.

Networking . . .

We genealogists network for a great many reasons . . . to find "living" relatives who wish to exchange family information . . . to share our research experience and expertise . . . to get past brick walls . . . to make other genealogists jump for joy. And we are some of the most kind and giving researchers around, since after all, our focus is on family. You'll find even more suggestions for networking in the textbook, **Fundamentals of Genealogy®: The Most Helpful Tools You've Never Used**.

🌿 When you say **"Networking"** to a genealogist today, you could mean Advertising, Blogs, Chat Rooms, Columns, Conferences, Database Providers, DNA Cousins, Family Holiday, Family Stories, Genealogical & Historical Societies, Mailing Lists, Message Boards, Newsletters, Periodicals, Photo & Video Sharing, Social Media (Facebook, Instagram, Pinterest, Twitter, etc.), Reunions, Seminars, Your Website and more!

🌿 **"Standards for Use of Technology in Genealogical Research,"** by the (U.S.) National Genealogical Society's "Standards and Guidelines" are at www.ngsgenealogy.org/cs/ngs_standards_and_guidelines

🌿 **"Standards for Publishing Web Pages on the Internet,"** by the (U.S.) National Genealogical Society's "Standards and Guidelines" are at www.ngsgenealogy.org/cs/ngs_standards_and_guidelines

🌿 **"Sharing Information with Others,"** by the (U.S.) National Genealogical Society's "Standards and Guidelines" are at www.ngsgenealogy.org/cs/ngs_standards_and_guidelines

🌿 Recommended **Blogs** for genealogists:
- The grand-daddy of finding genealogy blogs is Thomas MacEntee's **Geneabloggers** www.geneabloggers.com/
- Family Tree Magazine reviews the best genealogy blogs www.familytreemagazine.com/article/best-genealogy-blogs-2015
- See CyndisList "Blog" www.cyndislist.com/cyndislistsearch/?q=blog
- **Ancestry.com blog** http://blogs.ancestry.com/ancestry/
- **Board for the Certification of Genealogists' blog called Springboard** http://blog.bcgcertification.org/
- **DearMYRTLE's Genealogy Blog** http://blog.dearmyrtle.com/
- **Eastman's Online Genealogy Newsletter** http://blog.eogn.com
- **FamilySearch Blog** https://familysearch.org/blog/en/
- **Family Tree Magazine Blogs** www.familytreemagazine.com/Blogs/
  - **Genealogy Insider**, to help with your genealogy projects http://blog.familytreemagazine.com/insider/
  - **Photo Detective**, with Maureen A. Taylor, genealogy expert http://blog.familytreemagazine.com/photodetectiveblog/

- The Federation of Genealogical Societies' Blog called **FGS Voice** http://voice.fgs.org/
- **Fold3's Blog** http://blog.fold3.com/
- **Genealogy Blog Finder** http://blogfinder.Genealogue.com
- **The Indepth Genealogist Blog** http://theindepthgenealogist.com/blog/
- Judy G. Russell, JD, CG, CGL's Blog called **The Legal Genealogist** www.legalgenealogist.com/blog/
- **The National Archives Blog list** (U.S.) www.archives.gov/social-media/blogs.html
- The National Genealogical Society's Blog called **Upfront with NGS** http://upfront.ngsgenealogy.org/
- **Newberry Library's Genealogy Blog** www.newberry.org/genealogy-blog
- **"What's Up Genealogy?"**'s 4YourFamilyStory Blog https://www.4yourfamilystory.com/blog

🕸 **Crowdsourcing** – don't forget the Ancestry®'s good ole free **Electronic Mailing Lists** at RootsWeb http://lists.rootsweb.ancestry.com/ and the **Electronic Message Boards** of Ancestry®'s subsidiary RootsWeb at http://boards.rootsweb.com/ and of Genealogy.com at GenForum http://genforum.genealogy.com/ *(subscription service).*

🕸 **DNA - Networking with Database Cousins** – find suggestions at CyndisList "DNA, Genetics & Family Health" www.cyndislist.com/dna/

- **WikiTree** https://www.wikitree.com/ "We are a community of genealogists working together to grow an accurate single family tree using DNA and traditional genealogical sources."

🕸 **Facebook** – for more suggestions, see *the textbook, **Fundamentals of Genealogy®: The Most Helpful Tools You've Never Used**.*

- Katherine Wilson's guide lists hundreds of **genealogy-related Facebook pages** at https://moonswings.files.wordpress.com/2016/08/genealogy-on-facebook-list-03-august-2016.pdf. Thanks, Katherine!
- **Want to find genealogy groups on Facebook?** On your personal page, type the keyword "genealogy" in the search box, then you'll see a Results Types Ribbon under the search box so click "Group" to see the group search results. You'll see hundreds of genealogy groups! Further refine your search by typing more keywords in to the search box. When you've found a group you'd like to join, simply click the Join button on that group's page. Some Facebook groups are public (anyone can Join and read the page posts immediately) and others require an administrator to accept your request. Good luck!

- ❦ **Family Reunions** - Suggestions using today's tools:
  - Try a **Reunion App** like the ones at https://familysearch.org/apps/
  - Use Social Media platforms for **family group communication.**
  - **Share** your family history in person and electronically.
  - Build an **interactive family tree** at https://www.geni.com/
  - Find hundreds of Family Tree Magazine **reunion articles** for ways to prep, collection information, determine relationships, etc. www.family treemagazine.com/articlesearch/L0?SearchTerm=reunion&Sort=Rank
  - **CyndisList**:
    - "Newsletters" www.cyndislist.com/cyndislistsearch/?q=newsletter
    - "Recipes, Cookbooks & Family Traditions" www.cyndislist.com/recipes.htm
    - "Reunions" www.cyndislist.com/reunions.htm
- ❦ **Family Stories** and family lore can provide us with some of the best "clues" to begin our research . . . it should not be considered "fact" until we've proven each detail with other credible sources.
  - CyndisList **"Oral History & Interviews"** http://cyndislist.com/oral
- ❦ *See "**Important U.S. Genealogical & Historical Societies**" section.*
- ❦ **Genealogy Apps** for computers and smartphones:
  - **Ancestry.com Apps** www.ancestry.com/cs/ancestry-app page currently offers **The Ancestry, FindAGrave** and **Shoebox Apps** for using your smartphone as a scanner. **We're Related App** www.ancestry.com/wererelated/share/
  - An example **Facebook Apps** page https://www.facebook .com/search/apps/?q=family%20tree%20app
  - For **Facebook App Support Groups:**
    - Type the app name in the **Search** box, after results appear, in the line below the Search box click "Group."
    - Join the **"Genealogy – Apps Group"** https://www. facebook.com/groups/Genealogyapps/
    - Join the **"Genealogy App Development Test Group"** https://www.facebook.com/groups/genappdevtesters/
  - **The Family Nexus** http://thefamilynexus.com/
  - **FamilySearch App Gallery** https://familysearch.org/apps/ has a page full of free and paid apps.
  - **FindAGrave** app http://www.findagrave.com/mobileapp/ allows most website activities plus many new ones like the ability to upload a tombstone photo from your smartphone directly to the corresponding FindAGrave page. And more!
  - Is there a genealogy app for that? **Google search** 2 terms = any genealogy website or function + the word "App."

- Does your **local library** for its own app? Check the website!
- To learn about using the latest technology for genealogy on your smartphone, tablet or computer, read Lisa Louise Cooke's ***Mobile Genealogy: How to Use Your Tablet and Smartphone for Family History Research***.
- **Pinterest App Store** https://www.pinterest.com/appstore/
  - How to install iPhone and iPad Apps from Pinterest App Pins https://blog.pinterest.com/en/install-best-new-iphone-and-ipad-apps-pinterest
- **Reunion Touch** http://www.leisterpro.com/reuniontouch/ (paid) for iPhone, iPad and iPod Touch.
- **Saving Memories Forever** https://itunes.apple.com/ us/app/saving-memories-forever/id526117837?mt=8 (subscription) for smartphones, iPad and iPod Touch.
- **Stories, etc.** http://storiesetc.com/ (for Apple products) create videos, audio recordings, etc., and share them including on Facebook!

🖐 **Social Media** – becoming genealogists' answers + help powerhouse
  - **Family Tree Magazine's** "Find Genealogy Help on Social Media" www.familytreemagazine.com/article/genealogy-help-on-social-media
  - **When requesting information** on Social Media, fully identify your ancestor (give their full name and BMDD . . . for complete details, see the textbook ***Fundamentals of Genealogy®: Basics for Everyone***), tell how you knew to contact this person (like you saw their family tree online) and ask specifically for what you need (don't ask them "for all of their information.")

🖐 **Twitter** https://twitter.com/ Remember the entire world can see your tweets, usually finding them by hashtag or subject keywords.
  - **How to Begin**
    1. Set up a profile, find your Tribe (search for genealogy friends and organizations – more about this below) and follow them.
    2. Understand hashtags (labels beginning with the character # that allows the world to find tweets with that hashtag).
    3. Understand @Name (simply, you can tweet directly to another user's account by including their @Name in the tweet).
  - **Five Set Up Basics**
    1. Your profile should include some kind of photo or image otherwise they say, "No photo = No followers."
    2. Your profile should include a link to your website, Facebook, Instagram, Pinterest, LinkedIn, etc.
    3. Create a short bio emphasizing your genealogy interest.
    4. Create a short, easy to remember User Name.

5. Start by tweeting a few tweets with a #genealogy hashtag or two.

- **Find Who to Follow . . . and Find Followers**
  1. You can choose to find and follow those people in your stored contacts from email, Facebook, Instagram, Pinterest, LinkedIn, etc.
  2. Search for your favorite genealogy people and organizations.
  3. If you have kindred spirit with one, like a Local Genealogy Society, "Follow" everyone on their followers list . . . this will likely get you many tweeters who following you back!
  4. Go to Twellow.com https://twellow.com/splash/ Yellow Pages for ideas about "Who to Follow" or how to get more followers.

- **What to Tweet**
  1. Tweet about what interests you! (FYI---people aren't really interested in what you ate for dinner.)
  2. Tweet about a genealogy lecture or conference you're at using their hashtag. Find vendor specials at that conference using the hashtag.
  3. Share! If you just read something interesting, give a quick opinion or recommendation and include a URL.

🌿 *You'll find even more suggestions for networking in the textbook,* ***Fundamentals of Genealogy®: The Most Helpful Tools You've Never Used****.*

Preservation . . .

You can find lots of suggestions for preservation in the genealogy community with the advent of technology. If you can, make preservation a priority!

🌿 A comprehensive summary of how to start **DIGITALLY preserving** your genealogical materials on the FamilySearch blog, "Preserving Your Family History Records Digitally" https://familysearch.org/blog/en/?s=%22 Preserving+Your+Family+History+Records+Digitally%22

🌿 An easy **preservation trick** to do immediately --- go thru your heirloom papers and remove paper clips, staples (bend back folded prongs with tweezers), rubber bands, etc. Eliminate the need for these by placing the paper in flat-laying archival quality plastic sleeves or containers.

🌿 **Customized archival quality solutions** at www.Gaylord.com, https://www.familyarchives.com and www.ExposuresOnline.com
- **Archival Boxes & Supplies**
- **Climate Control Supplies** https://www.familyarchives.com/ categories/Archival-Boxes-%26-Supplies/Climate-Control/
- **Humidity Cards**
- **Hydrothermograph**

- **Silica Gel**
- General advice for **protecting your heirlooms**:
  - For **bronze and metal items**, etc., naturally develop a patina (a surface film) that should not be disturbed since it speaks to the item's quality and integrity over time. Removing patina could devalue it. When cleaning, gently vacuum or dust so not to disturb the patina.
  - Remember to **catalog your heirlooms**, treating them like the information you would gather for an insurance claim . . . list full description, provenance of ownership, value, significance to the family and where it's physically located today.
  - For **ceramics**, while especially durable, they do need special protection again scratching, breakage, cracking, etc., when packing in storage. Clean with a clean, damp cloth.
  - **Glass items** are typically chemically stable and primarily at risk of cracking, breaking and chipping. Sunlight might diminish them. To clean them gently, use water with a mild detergent (unless the glass also has materials that will be ruined with water, like paper labels, washable inks, etc.).
  - **Silver articles** are prone to surface tarnishing which is best removed by polishing gently with a silver cleaner and drying thoroughly with a soft cloth. Commercial dip solutions are not recommended.
  - To protect your **heirloom textiles**, remember that the fibers in any cloth will eventually begin to disintegrate. To lengthen their life, research the type of fabric and seek professional advice.
- General advice for **dealing with the environmental elements**:
  - **Excessive dryness** can cause wood and ivory items to become brittle and crack with time. They must be stored with climate controlled supplies . . . see "Customized archival quality solutions" above.
  - To counteract **moisture** that might damage paper and other items, by saving or buying the **Silica Gel Packs** (that are often sold with shoes). They remove moisture and are ideal to store with papers that become damaged by moisture, like photos and other paper heirlooms.
  - Pests, like many insects, can be dissuaded from your heirlooms with natural products and remedies. Google your heirloom's material composition and find expert advice on what natural product or remedy you should use to accompany your heirloom storage.
  - **Sunlight** damages most delicate items, so make it a habit to keep them out of direct sunlight and to cover all paper items with black cloth or sunlight-proof protection (like 3-ring binders sitting on a bookshelf near a window).
- Suggestions for **preserving newspaper clippings**:

- **Neutralize the newspaper's own acid content** to stop it becoming yellow or brittle by using a recommended spray like Bookkeeper or Archival Mist (they contain an alkaline solution with methoxyl magnesium methyl carbonate).
- **Digitize** them for everyday use and a second form of preservation.
- Consider how **environmental elements** react with the newspaper – avoid sunlight, moisture, extreme temperatures, etc. (*see Climate Control above*).
- **Store the newspaper properly** – individually within "archival quality" storage (acid-free and lignen-free), without folding, paper clips, staples, tape, rubber bands, etc.
- Place the **source citation** along with the storage materials.

How about preserving your **family's cultural traditions**? Understanding our ancestors' clothing, language, food, music, religion, stories, artifacts, dances, gatherings, holidays, etc., can give us ideas for how to create our own ways of observing and keeping these traditions alive today.

How should you **display, preserve and store paper photos**? Advice from the FamilySearch blog "**Family History Preservation: Preserving Family Photos**" (referencing NARA webpages, "How to Preserve Family Papers and Photographs" and "Preserving Family Photos.")

- **Labeling Photos** --- "A photo without a name quickly becomes meaningless and can easily get thrown out or tossed into a box in the basement and forgotten . . . Remember that markers and ink can damage photos. Try writing on the back of the photos with pencil. If the photo won't accept pencil, use an acid-free scrapbooking pen to write on the back, in the margin, or on an accompanying plastic sleeve. Include in the label the names of the people in the photos and information about the event, location, and date."
- **Displaying Photos** --- "Nearly every family has photos hanging on their walls and arranged in books or albums on shelves. A few simple steps can help keep your photos safe while you display them:
  - Display a copy and store the original whenever possible.
  - Keep photos out of direct sunlight.
  - Use photo corners instead of glue or tape to mount photos.
  - Use acid-free, archival safe albums and books for photos."
- **Preserve Photos** --- "Scanning and saving your photos to your computer creates important, versatile backups. Digitizing photos also allows you to restore and share them. Specialized software can help even out the coloring and correct faded or dark spots and patch together torn sections. You can hire a professional to do these tasks, or

you can attempt them yourself. Read FamilySearch's series **Restoring Damaged Photographs** to learn how."

- **Store Photos** --- "Store photos in cool, dry places to protect them from mold, insects, and hot temperatures that can cause them to discolor, curl, or stick together. If you do have extremely damaged photos (such as from insects or mold), weigh how important the photos are to you and then consider calling a conservator. Store slides in their carousels in boxes to protect them from dust and light. If you must touch photographs, negatives, or slides, wear gloves. Damaging substances on your hands can cause permanent stains."

🌿 How should you **preserve today's digital photos files and docs**?

- **Digital Photos** --- 1) Immediately transfer your smartphone photos to a digital storage location (like your computer or cloud storage, 2) Save them to today's current digital storage solution (like a flash drive), and 3) Think about making today's version of the old family portrait our ancestors had – do you have the equivalent to pass down to future generations? If not, immediately take some family portrait photos.
- Try an app like **Chatbooks** https://chatbooks.com/ to store & present!
- **Digital Files and Documents** --- Use today's latest technology for creating lasting digital files and expect to upgrade to the latest new digital storage solutions when it comes along.

🌿 *For more preservation ideas, see the textbook, **Fundamentals of Genealogy®: The Most Helpful Tools You've Never Used**.*

Presentations . . .
After spending the time researching, you deserve to have some fun, creative ways to share your genealogy projects!

🌿 Kimberly Powell shares LOTS of **good paper and digital presentation ideas** at ThoughtCo's "Genealogy" section https://www.thoughtco.com/genealogy-4133308. Topics include "Photos, Scrapbooking & Memorabilia" and "Writing and Publishing Your Family History."

🌿 Helen McKenna's free Kindle, **"You Can Write Your Life Story"** https://www.amazon.com/dp/B00AR7_Z0ZG/ref=as_li_ss_tl?ie=UTF8&linkCode=sl1&tag=geneabloggers-20&linkId=f04f53a7b6910bcbed69aa_5fcf8d5ed6

🌿 **Animoto** https://www.Animoto.com --- Try fun and free video creation with a very easy interface experience. This free program allows you to write narration plus upload images and video to their graphic video templates (that also includes their music). If you like the free features, you can upgrade to an annual paid membership at three different price/features levels. Animoto is ideal for many genealogical projects, especially those for digital scrapbooks.

🌿 **BYBU's "Ancestors"** tv series online resources include:
  - **"Writing Your History"** at www.byub.org/ancestors/records/familyhistory/intro2.html
  - **"Publishing Your Family History"** at www.byub.org/ancestors/records/familyhistory/intro3.html

🌿 Present your family history by **self-publishing** your own books in paper and digital formats using today's technology!
  - Add your story, photos, research, documents, etc., in to a word processing or note-taking program to create a digital file that you can upload to many places such as a digital book (some below) and/or photocopy for a paper book.
  - Do the same as above with only photo or document images.
  - Try a smartphone app like **Chatbooks** https://chatbooks.com/ to create photo albums directly from your smartphone or tablet photos!
  - Upload your photo or document image files to an online book creation company like:
    ▪ **Shutterfly** https://www.shutterfly.com/
    ▪ **CVS Photo** www.cvs.com/photo
  - Self-publish your book with a professional service like:
    ▪ **Lulu** https://www.lulu.com/
    ▪ **Blurb** www.blurb.com

🌿 **EasyBib** www.easybib.com free software tool for generating source citations in MLA, APA, Chicago and other formats.

🌿 **Facebook** https://www.facebook.com --- *See the "Facebook" section of Fundamentals of Genealogy®: The Most Helpful Tools You've Never Used for ideas about sharing your genealogical projects online with family, especially uploading your digital photos to a Facebook Photo Album in the "Photos" section.*

🌿 **Family Book Creator** www.familybookcreator.com/en/ --- Genealogists are raving about this one! Try this plug-in to the Family Tree Maker software (for Windows) plus Microsoft Word to create books from the research you've already entered into Family Tree Maker in just a few clicks. Visit their website for examples of family data books, family charts, genealogy reports including incorporating your photos and image files. It's currently available in English and Spanish.

🌿 Create a **Family Cookbook**! For more ideas, see CyndisList "Cookbook" listings www.cyndislist.com/cyndislistsearch/?q=cookbook

🌿 **FamilySearch Family Trees** https://familysearch.org/tree --- Post your family tree to a free reputable online lineage collection, like FamilySearch

Family Trees. Not only can your relatives find this information and add to it (depending on how you set the privacy settings) but others can benefit from your accurate research.

- 🌿 **GEDCOM-to-Webpage Conversion Software**, see CyndsList page www.cyndislist.com/gedcom/gedcom-to-web-page-conversion/
- 🌿 Lisa Alzo's "**Genealogy Intensive: The Write Stuff**" www.genea bloggers.com/announcing-write-stuff-genealogy-intensive-offering/
- 🌿 Tips from FamilySearch Blog for **getting the next generation** involved:
  - "Creating Traditions That Make Family Memories" https://familysearch.org/blog/en/creating-traditions-family-memories/
  - "Preserve the Stories of Grandparents Forever with These Expert Tips" https://familysearch.org/blog/en/preserve-stories-grandparents-expert-tips/
  - "Too Young For Family History? Think Again!" https://familysearch.org/blog/en/young-family-history/
- 🌿 Want more **Gift** ideas? See "Gifts of Research" in *Fundamentals of Genealogy®: The Most Helpful Tools You've Never Used*.
- 🌿 **HistoryLines** https://historylines.com/ instant family history.
- 🌿 **"Large Family Tree Wall Decal"** to add your enlarged family portrait photos (currently on Amazon.com for US$10) also called "DIY Photo Gallery Frame Decor Sticker By LaceDecaL"
- 🌿 Give the gift of health and create a Medical Family Tree . . . *see the* ***"Summary of Today's Medical Family Tree and Predisposition Results Sheet'*** *section (pages 15-22).*
- 🌿 **Memory Box for family heirlooms** --- Find an archival quality box to place family heirlooms into, like a family bible, for safe storage and heirloom status. One idea is at a company called Exposures.com where they can personalize storage, like a "Memory Box" whose lid you can customize with an image, perhaps a family tree showing how the family bible that is protected inside was passed down thru the family http://search.exposuresonline.com/search?p=Q&ts=custom&w=memory +box. For any heirloom, make it easy for future generations to see the provenance, ownership and inheritance --- preserve it properly and include a record of all of its family history information.
- 🌿 **Scrapbooking - Digital** --- Here are several ideas:
  - **Let a book help you** --- Type "digital genealogy scrapbook" into Amazon.com's search function and you'll find several choices. Once you've found one that sounds like the help you're looking for, save yourself some money and see whether your library's inter-library loan can let you loan it in paper or digital form. *See the "Libraries" section*

in *Fundamentals of Genealogy®: The Most Helpful Tools You've Never Used.*

- Using an **ancestral database software program** --- Genealogists often overlook the obvious by not exploring the presentation options of their ancestral database software program. Many charts can be saved as a digital file that can be added to your digital scrapbook. Is that a natural fit for your scrapbook? *See the "Software" section.*
- If you love **Evernote or OneNote**, try creating a category and downloading digital files into it. Both of these programs allow you to instantly create a book by exporting your pages within a category tab!

🌿 **Scrapbooking - Paper** --- Here are several ideas:

- **Let a book help you** --- Type "scrapbooking" into Amazon.com's search function and you'll find many choices. Once you've found one that sounds like the help you're looking for, save yourself some money and see whether your library's inter-library loan can let you loan it in paper or digital form. *See this book's "Libraries" section in* ***Fundamentals of Genealogy®: The Most Helpful Tools You've Never Used***.
- Using an **ancestral database software program** --- Genealogists often overlook the obvious by not exploring the presentation options of their ancestral database software program. Many charts can be printed and added to your paper scrapbook. *See the "Software" section in* ***Fundamentals of Genealogy®: The Most Helpful Tools You've Never Used***.
- Trying to **remove paper photos** from an adhesive photo album? Forget the steam. Try dental floss!

🌿 **Share** your family tree on a popular genealogy website like:

- **Ancestry.com** Member Family Tree https://www.ancestry.com/
- **MyHeritage** Family Tree Builder https://www.myheritage.com/
- **TribalPages** Family Trees www.tribalpages.com/tpshowcase.html
- **WikiTree's** Free Family Tree https://www.wikitree.com/

🌿 Want to start a **Website** for your family history? See section called **"Website of Your Own for genealogy"** in the ***Fundamentals of Genealogy®: The Most Helpful Tools You've Never Used***.

🌿 Write your family's own **Who Do You Think You Are** story www.whodoyouthinkyouarestory.com/

🌿 See **CyndisList** http://www.cyndislist.com by searching with keywords corresponding to your question.

🌿 *Find more ideas in* ***Fundamentals of Genealogy®: The Most Helpful Tools You've Never Used***.

Bibliography and Recommended Reading . . .

Board for Certification of Genealogists. *The BCG Genealogical Standards Manual.* Washington, D.C., U.S.A.: Ancestry Publishing, 2014.

* ~ Eichholz, Alice (editor). *Red Book.* 3rd revised edition. Washington, D.C., U.S.A.: Ancestry Publishing, 2004.

FitzHugh, Terrick V.H. *The Dictionary of Genealogy* 5th edition. London, England, United Kingdom: S &C Black (Publishers) Limited, 1998.

~ Greenwood, Val D. *The Researcher's Guide to American Genealogy.* 3rd edition. Baltimore, Maryland, USA: Genealogical Publishing Co, 2013.

Jones, Thomas W. *Mastering Genealogical Proof.* Arlington, Virginia, U.S.A.: National Genealogical Society, 2013.

Mills, Elizabeth Shown. *Evidence! Citation & Analysis for the Family Historian.* Baltimore, Maryland: Genealogical Publishing Co., 2011.

Mills, Elizabeth Shown. *Evidence Explained: Citing History Sources from Artifacts to Cyberspace.* 3rd edition. Baltimore, Maryland, U.S.A.: Genealogical Publishing Company, 2015.

~ Peterson-Maass, Marsha. *Fundamentals of Genealogy®: Basics for Everyone.* Lulu Publishing Company www.Lulu.com, 2017.

Peterson-Maass, Marsha. *Fundamentals of Genealogy®: Beyond Shaky Leaf Hints.* Lulu Publishing Company www.Lulu.com, 2017.

Peterson-Maass, Marsha. *Fundamentals of Genealogy®: Medical Family Tree Workbook.* Lulu Publishing Company www.Lulu.com, 2017.

Peterson-Maass, Marsha. *Fundamentals of Genealogy®: The Most Helpful Tools You've Never Used.* Lulu Publishing Company www.Lulu.com, 2017.

Rose, Christine. *Genealogical Proof Standard: Building a Solid Case.* San Jose, California, U.S.A.: CR Publications, 2005.

Schaeffer, Mark W. *The Tao of Twitter: Changing Your Life and Business 140 Characters at a Time.* New York, NY: McGraw Hill Education, 2014.

Smith, Drew. *Social Networking for Genealogists.* Baltimore, Maryland, U.S.A.: Genealogical Publishing Company, 2009.

* ~ Szucs, Loretto Dennis and Sandra Hargreaves Luebking. *The Source: A Guidebook of American Genealogy.* 3rd edition. Salt Lake City, Utah, U.S.A.: Ancestry Inc., 2006.

* Currently available for free online (in part or whole) at Ancestry® Wiki http://ancestry.com/wiki or Google Books https://books.google.com/

~ Recommended for **Record Groups** research.

Fundamentals of Genealogy®: Basics for Everyone

Second edition, part of the *Fundamentals of Genealogy*® textbook series

Appendix A: Create Your Own Genealogy Library . . .

Whether in paper or digital form (find some online for free, see the textbooks with an asterisk on page 99), begin building your genealogy library today. Here are some recommendations for all levels of genealogists.

- All publications listed in "***Bibliography and Recommended Reading***."
- Bettinger, Blaine T. ***The Family Tree Guide to DNA Testing and Genetic Genealogy.*** Cincinnati, Ohio, U.S.A.: Family Tree Books, 2016.
- Smith, Drew. ***Organize Your Genealogy: Strategies and Solutions for Every Researcher.*** Cincinnati, Ohio, U.S.A.: Family Tree Books, 2016.
- Levenick, Denise May. ***How to Archive Family Keepsakes.*** Cincinnati, Ohio, U.S.A.: Family Tree Books, 2012.

Appendix B: *Fundamentals of Genealogy*® Research Strategies . . .

*Best wishes using the **Fundamentals of Genealogy**® research strategies!®*

***Fundamentals of Genealogy*® Research Strategy, "Beginning Genealogy – How Do I Get Started?"** Just beginning your genealogical journey? Begin with a complete overview of accredited genealogical methods and project organization!
- Find the overview on pages 3-4, "**Checklist-Start With Accredited Methods.**"
- Visit http://fundamentalsofgenealogy.blogspot.com/ for downloadable charts!
- *Explore the Record types in the **"Basic U.S. Genealogical Record Group."***
  - Make sure to take the next step in understanding genealogical Record Groups and sources by reading Loretto Dennis Szucs and Sandra Hargreaves Luebking's **The Source: A Guidebook to American Genealogy** (copyright and published in 1997, Ancestry Publishing, Provo, Utah) . . . *see the "Wiki" section to view it for free at Ancestry®'s Wiki.*
- **"Recommended Genealogical Records/Resources Database Providers."**
- Remember to not only research online . . . make a site visit to a location where your ancestors lived and get your hands dirty in their local records . . . *see the* **"Important U.S. National & State Genealogical Libraries, Repositories and Archives"** *(pages 24-26) and* **"How to Find U.S. National, State & LOCAL Genealogical Repositories"** *(pages 26-27) for some prep ideas.*
- **"Appendix A: Create Your Own Genealogy Library"** *for recommendations.*
- Begin recording information you already have and begin citing your sources in the accredited methodology . . . see **Fundamentals of Genealogy®: Basics for Everyone** for formatting.
- Make an inventory of your family's precious heirlooms.
- Find the database software that's right for you . . . *see the "Software" section.*
- *See the "Organization" section for ideas how to start with a bang!*
- Educate yourself further with these articles, videos and webinars:
  - **About.com's "One Stop Beginner's Genealogy"**
    http://genealogy.about.com/library/onestop/bl_beginner.htm

- **Ancestry.com's Learning Center (U.S.)**
  www.ancestrylibrary.com/cs/HelpAndAdviceUS
  - ✓ **YouTube Channel** https://www.youtube.com/user/AncestryCom
  - ✓ **Ancestry Academy** https://www.ancestry.com/academy/
- **DearMYRTLE's lessons** http://blog.dearmyrtle.com/
  - • **YouTube Channel** https://www.youtube.com/user/DearMYRTLE
  - • **Webinars** http://blog.dearmyrtle.com/p/geneawebinars-calendar.html
- **FamilySearch Learning Center**
  https://familysearch.org/learningcenter/home.html
  - ✓ **"Simple Start to Family History"** https://familysearch.org/blog/en/simple-start-family-history-2/?prclt=rJE8KK3V
  - ✓ **YouTube Channel** https://www.youtube.com/user/familysearch
- **National Genealogical Society's Educational Courses**
  www.ngsgenealogy.org/cs/educational_courses

***Fundamentals of Genealogy*® Research Strategy, "Brick Walls – Strategies For Breaking Thru"** . . . do any of these proven methods help you break thru?

🐚 **"He just up and disappeared."** Have you made an **exhaustive search in local records** (this is part of the Genealogical Proof Standard) . . . *see "Research Strategy, "Conflicting Information - How Do I Resolve It?"* below.

🐚 **Researching Common Names.** Make sure to fully "Identity" your ancestor *(page 6)*, "**Re-analyze**" *(below)* and download this Rootsweb outline from Drew Smith, MLS, **"Your Ancestor's FAN Club: Using Cluster Research to Get Past Brick Walls"** www.rootsweb.ancestry.com/~fljgstb/Presentations/2016NovemberPresentation.pdf

🐚 **Overcome Surname Changes** . . . *see "Researching Female Ancestors."*

🐚 **Only one search strategy** (lately it might be "online only research") . . . *see the other Research Strategies, paying close attention to "Rounding Up the Usual Suspects" and "Rounding Up BEYOND the Usual Suspects."*

🐚 **Re-analyze** all of your clues.
- • **Correctly analyze all of your info**, especially Obits and Census (do you understand every word, every clue to investigate, all people and relationships?).
- • **Assumptions** – Separate facts from assumptions and re-analyze your case without the assumptions. Not sure how to do this? Ask another researcher to start at the beginning and list the facts.
- • **County Boundaries** – Review each town's county boundaries at the time your ancestors lived there to know the correct county offices to request your ancestors' records from. Use Newberry Library's Atlas of Historic County Boundaries http://publications.newberry.org/ahcbp/.
- • Find **Records Substitutes** when "the courthouse burned down" – start with USGenWeb www.usgenweb.org/ and FamilySearch Wiki. http://familysearch.org/wiki for finding extant local sources.
- • Use a biography-based **Timeline** of an ancestor's life events to find gaps in research, progression of residential locations and possible motivations for

their actions. If you've loaded your research into an genealogy database software program can you easily create one?

- Can't find the answer about whether a source exists or what to do if the courthouse burned down or just about anything else? **Network** to get the answer! See the *"Networking"* section.
- Make a **Site Visit** to your ancestor's birthplace or contact a local society.
- Have you searched the **IGI**? https://familysearch.org/wiki/en/International_ Genealogical_Index
- **Hire a Professional Genealogist** . . . see *"Some Basic Research Tools."*
🐚 *Find even more advice for your everyday research in **Fundamentals of Genealogy®: The Most Helpful Tools You've Never Used**.*

Fundamentals of Genealogy® Research Strategy, "Conflicting Information - How Do I Resolve It?"

🐚 As we're researching and gathering a Body of Information, we'll find conflicting information since we're gathering it (hopefully) from different sources. We must **weigh each piece of evidence for its credibility** and go with the piece of evidence possessing the strongest weight . . . see the *"**Analysis**"* section.

🐚 Focus on building your Body of Information with the step from the Genealogical Proof Standard called, "**Reasonably Exhaustive Search**." Read Judy Russell's BCG Skillbuilding article, "DNA and the Reasonably Exhaustive Search" *OnBoard* 20 (January 2014):1-2, 7 at www.bcgcertification.org/skillbuilders/index.html . . . *and also see the "**Genealogy Analysis Style Sheet**" section.*

🐚 For an accredited approach to this common research issue, see Thomas Jones' book, ***Mastering Genealogical Proof***, in which he explains the "Genealogical Proof Standard" and devotes Chapter 6 to this topic, "GPS Element 4: Resolving Conflicts and Assembling Evidence."

Fundamentals of Genealogy® Research Strategy, "Female Ancestors – Researching For Maiden Names" (in patrilineal/patronymic naming convention):

🐚 Helpful Record Types for the married surname change:
- (Their children's) **Birth Records**
- **Census Records** (their parents might reside there)
- (Their and their children's) **Death Records**
- **Marriage Records**
- (Their husband's) **Military Pension Records**
- (Their, husband's, parents') **Naturalization Records**
- (Their parents and siblings') **Obituaries**
- **Religious Records**
- **School Records**
- **U.S. Social Security Application Records**
- (Their children's) **U.S. Social Security SS-5 Form**
- **Wills and Probate Records**
🐚 Locate her in U.S. Federal Censuses. Are her parents living with her married family? Browse neighbors. Did she move and certain neighbors move with her?

❧ Could her middle name or her children's first and middle names be clues to her parents' names and surname?

❧ Who were the informants on her records?

❧ *Find more advice in* **Fundamentals of Genealogy®: The Most Helpful Tools You've Never Used**.

Fundamentals of Genealogy® Research Strategy, "First Finding Sources"
Sometimes we begin research on an individual with little more information than a name and possibly a time period. As genealogists, we work from the known to the unknown. If we could only find that first clue that helps direct us toward their identity. First Finding Sources give us these possible "identity candidates."

❧ **Censuses** . . . *see the* **"Census Records"** *section.*

❧ **Directories, Phone Books or Online White Pages Websites** . . . *see* **"Directory Records – U.S. City, County and Phone"** *section.*

❧ **Military Records** . . . *see the* **"Military Records"** *section.*

❧ **Obituary and Newspaper Records** . . . . . . *see* **"Newspaper Records."**

❧ **U.S. Social Security Death Index** (available at FamilySearch.org and Ancestry.com) and **U.S. Social Security Applications and Claims Index** (available at Ancestry.com).

❧ **Tax Records** . . . *see the* **"Tax Records"** *section.*

❧ Consult these **other sources** (for both the Subject and their known relatives) that might give many more life details, like:
  • **Biographical Sketches** and **Compiled Lineages**
  • **Death Records**, including cemetery records, will/probate, etc.
  • **Family Records**
  • **Marriage Records**
  • **Military Records**
  • **Naturalization and Immigration Records**
  • **Religious Records**

❧ If you know a possible location and time period, find **Maps and Gazetteers** at that time . . . *see* **"Maps and Gazetteers"** *in the* **"Some Basic Tools."** *section.*

❧ Look for your Immigrant Ancestor and other family members in paper and online **Guides** of extant records for the possible city, town, parish, village, etc.

Fundamentals of Genealogy® Research Strategy, "New Year's Resolution Suggestions"

❧ Can you work on a **Brick Wall** using some suggestions above?

❧ Can you make a **copy of your digital files** for safe keeping?

❧ Can you reach out to **DNA Database Cousins** to check lineages?

❧ Can you make a **family heirlooms inventory** if one doesn't yet exist?

❧ Can you take the **"Fundamentals of Genealogy® Organizational Challenge"** in the **"Organization"** section above?

❧ Can you check the **"Important U.S. National & State Gen. Libraries, Repositories and Archives"** to find any **new features**?

❧ Can you investigate a new **presentation** style for your research?

- Can you try a *Fundamentals of Genealogy®* **Research Strategy**?
- Can you **share** some of your research from this last year?
- Can you make a **site visit** to a repository or take a research trip?
- Can you try a new type of **Social Media Networking**?
- Can you put an ancestor's life events into a **Timeline** to create a bio?
- *Find even more advice for your everyday research in* **Fundamentals of Genealogy®: The Most Helpful Tools You've Never Used***.*

Fundamentals of Genealogy® Research Strategy, "Newly Found Ancestor - How Do I Begin Research On Newly Found Ancestor?"

- If you're a genealogy newbie, use the **Ancestral Profile** (pages 7-8) to guide you in which information to obtain from which records.
- Once you've identified your ancestor's possible residential location, try to find a **Map** for that location at that time and learn the **History** of events at that time since many records may have been created for your ancestors based on those events . . . *see* **"Local History"** *and* **"Maps and Gazetteers"** *in the* **"Basic Genealogical Tools"** *section.*
- Some suggested record types to seek at the beginning of your search:
  - Search for **Death Records** first, including U.S. Social Security records (for a recent ancestor), Obituaries, Death Certificate, Will/Probate, Cemetery records, etc. *See* **"Death Records"** *section.*
  - Search for other **Vital Records** . . . *see* **"Birth Records," "Divorce Records"** *and* **"Marriage Records"** *sections.*
  - Search for all **U.S. Federal Census** returns for their lifetime *. . . see* **"U.S. Census Records"** *section.*
- Once you believe you have a good handle on this ancestor's identity, search for previously published **Family Histories, Biographies**, other records types like **Military** records, etc.
- Not much info to begin with? see *Fundamentals of Genealogy®* **Research Strategy, "No Initial Information – How Do I Begin Researching If I Have Virtually No Information About My Ancestor?"** *(below).*
- See if there's a local genealogical or historical society and glean information from their website, Facebook, etc., or even join it. . . . *see the* **"Important U.S. Genealogical & Historical Societies"** *and* **"How to Find Other U.S. Organizations with local record collections"** *sections.*
- Look for your Immigrant Ancestor and other family members in paper and online **Guides** of extant records for the possible town, parish, village, etc.
- Do other *Fundamentals of Genealogy®* **Research Strategies** help you?

Fundamentals of Genealogy® Research Strategy, "No Initial Information – How Do I Begin Researching If I Have Virtually No Information About My Ancestor?"

- Remember that we research back one generation at a time, going from the known to the unknown, proving parental relationships before we go back another generation. Don't skip generations. *See the* **"Precepts"** *section.*

- Since you're working back one generation at a time, you will want to find clues that clearly state a parental relationship. For example, if you know that a son was named "Elisha Smith," but you have no info for his father, seek records for Elisha Smith that will likely state who his parents are, like a U.S. Social Security Application, Birth and Death Records, etc.
- Know that you're ultimately seeking Vital Records (Birth, Marriage, Divorce & Death records) to help prove your ancestor's identity. Make it a point to collect as much detailed vital event dates and locations. This will give you a timeframe in certain locations to search for extant records.
- *See the **Fundamentals of Genealogy**® Research Strategies, "First Finding Sources" and "Newly Found Ancestor - How Do I Begin Research On Newly Found Ancestor?" above.*

Fundamentals of Genealogy® Research Strategy, "Notetaking Software – A Format To Quicken, Organize And Record Your Research"

🐾 Try using the **Evernote/OneNote research recording format** below. For each Research Project, create a page ordered with these 3 sections:

TIMELINE OF ANCESTOR'S LIFE EVENTS
- Create a timeline with date at left, dot leader [. . . .] and description of the event including source citations.
- As you research your ancestor and fill in this timeline, you're also building a biographical timeline for that ancestor.
- Looking at this timeline can help quickly answer questions about past research to save time digging thru many paper files.

TO DO LIST
- As opportunities for further research arise from clues, add them.
- As these tasks are accomplished, highlight and use the "Strikeout" font feature (instead of deleting) to see what you've already done.

RESEARCH . . . in reverse chronological order (newest at top)
- This helps you know where you left off (since you'll place the newest research at the top of this section).
- Evernote and OneNote allow you to drop screen clippings into that project page that include the URL and date/time stamp below the clipping *(below)*.

Fundamentals of Genealogy® Research Strategy, "Notetaking Software - Using A Research Template"

🐾 When researching for biographical info, add the following Subject Headings (or one you develop yourself) to the top of your Evernote/OneNote digital file:
- **Timeline** [create a timeline of events below this subject heading]
- **Research Strategy**
- **Research Log**

🐾 **Digitized Documents, URLs and Source Citations**
- CyndisList **"Evernote Templates"** www.cyndislist.com/evernote/templates/
- *More Evernote and OneNote ideas are in **Fundamentals of Genealogy®: The Most Helpful Tools You've Never Used**.*

Fundamentals of Genealogy®: Basics for Everyone

Second edition, part of the *Fundamentals of Genealogy*® textbook series

Fundamentals of Genealogy® Research Strategy, "Rounding Up the Usual Suspects"

🌿 Simply put, make a list of the sources and websites you "usually" use at the beginning of a research project. Examples to get you started:
  - **Ancestry.com** https://www.ancestry.com/
  - **CyndisList** http://www.cyndislist.com/
  - **FamilySearch** https://familysearch.org/
  - **FamilySearch Books** https://books.familysearch.org/
  - **FamilySearch Wiki** https://familysearch.org/wiki/
  - **Google** https://www.google.com/
  - **Google Books** https://books.google.com/
  - **USGenWeb** http://www.usgenweb.org/
  - **VitalRec** http://www.vitalrec.com/
  - **WorldCat** http://www.worldcat.org/
🌿 *Find more advice in* **Fundamentals of Genealogy®: The Most Helpful Tools You've Never Used**.

Fundamentals of Genealogy® Research Strategy, "Rounding Up BEYOND the Usual Suspects"

🌿 Once you've compiled your "Usual Suspects" list *(above)*, as you're researching and checking those "usual" sources, make it a point to GO BEYOND and seek new sources. Here are a few tips to get you started:
  - Use the **Ancestral Profile** (pages 7-8)
  - *Check* **"Important U.S. National & State Gen. Libraries, Repositories and Archives."**
  - *Check* **"Recommended Gen. Records/Resources Database Providers."**
  - *Check* **"Recommended Genealogical Resources Organizations."**
  - *Check* **"Important U.S. Genealogical & Historical Societies."**
  - *Check* **"Recommended Educational Resources for gen. pursuits."**
  - *Check the* **"Networking"** *section.*
🌿 *Find more advice in* **Fundamentals of Genealogy®: The Most Helpful Tools You've Never Used**.

Appendix C: Excepts from *Fundamentals of Genealogy*®: *Beyond Shaky Leaf Hints* . . .

🌿 If you got your start in genealogy with an online provider like Ancestry® you may feel stuck wondering, **"What do I do next?"** Here are some suggestions to get you past your dependence on the shaky leaf hints.

- The FREE research process at FamilySearch is similar to Ancestry® but with many different records collections . . . *see **"FamilySearch"** within **"Recommended Gen. Records/Resources Database Providers."***
- Follow the ***Fundamentals of Genealogy*® Research Strategy, "Beginning Genealogy – How Do I Get Started?"**
- If you'd like a fun project where you find what you need at Ancestry® choose a U.S. ancestor from the 19th Century and try to find each **U.S. Federal Census enumeration for their life**. Download an image of each (including the source citation info), compile them and give it as a small paper or digital gift book to a family member who has never seen these details for your ancestor. Congrats on telling Ancestry® what to do!
- Can any of the other ***Fundamentals of Genealogy*® Research Strategies** in **"Appendix B"** help you?

🌿 If you're asking, **"Where do I go next?"**, then see the **"Important U.S. Public & Private Sources"** chapter with the **"Family Sources"** and **"U.S. National, State and Local Sources"** sections.

🌿 *Find even more advice in **Fundamentals of Genealogy®: The Most Helpful Tools You've Never Used***.

Made in United States
Orlando, FL
28 January 2023

29171634R00061